SEASONAL FOOD

A GUIDE TO WHAT'S IN SEASON WHEN AND WHY

www.booksattransworld.co.uk

SEASONAL FOOD

A GUIDE TO WHAT'S IN SEASON WHEN AND WHY

Paul Waddington

Photographs by Peter Williams

eden project books

Paul Waddington was born in Scunthorpe in 1964 and brought up in Chesterfield. He studied in Liverpool and Toulouse and then worked for Reuters and the *Financial Times* before setting up the writing agency Plain Text. He and his family live in Brixton.

TRANSWORLD PUBLISHERS
61–63 Uxbridge Road, London W5 5SA
a division of The Random House Group Ltd

RANDOM HOUSE AUSTRALIA (PTY) LTD
20 Alfred Street, Milsons Point, Sydney,
New South Wales 2061, Australia

RANDOM HOUSE NEW ZEALAND LTD
18 Poland Road, Glenfield, Auckland 10, New Zealand

RANDOM HOUSE SOUTH AFRICA (PTY) LTD
Endulini, 5a Jubilee Road, Parktown 2193, South Africa

Published 2004 by Eden Project Books
a division of Transworld Publishers

Copyright © Paul Waddington 2004
Photography by Peter Williams

The right of Paul Waddington to be identified as the author
of this work has been asserted in accordance with sections 77
and 78 of the Copyright, Designs and Patents Act 1988.

A catalogue record for this book is available from the British Library.
ISBN 1903 919525

The lines at the beginning of each month are taken from
The Shepherd's Calendar by John Clare (1793–1864)

Typeset in 11/14pt Adobe Caslon by
Falcon Oast Graphic Art Ltd

Printed in Italy by Graphicom

1 3 5 7 9 10 8 6 4 2

Papers used by Eden Project Books are natural, recyclable products made from wood
grown in sustainable forests. The manufacturing processes conform to the environmental
regulations of the country of origin.

For my mother and in memory of my father

Is there anybody out there who doesn't, in quiet moments,
feel in his or her heart that the future lies in working with the grain of nature?

Tim Smit, Eden Project

The correspondence between good farming, good nutrition and
great gastronomy is absolute, and wonderful.

Colin Tudge, *So Shall We Reap*

Contents

Acknowledgements

I would like to thank all the people who made this book possible: Karen MacLachlan for introducing me to my agent Sappho Clissitt; Sappho for her tireless promotion of the *Seasonal Food* idea; and Susanna Wadeson at Transworld for her encouragement, enthusiasm and for making it all happen. Thanks are also due to Deborah Adams and Alison Martin at Transworld, to Gavin Morris for his beautiful design, Peter Williams for his delicious photography, and to Mike Petty and the team at the Eden Project. Thank you too to Charlie Hicks for valuable vegetable advice, Garry Moen for insights into meat and game, Steve Hatt for fish facts and Mark Newman of Hamish Johnston for thoughts on British cheese. I am very grateful to Mary, Rosamund and Richard Young of Kite's Nest farm for their hospitality, for inspiration about farming, and for introducing me to the work of John Clare. I should also like to thank Adrian Evans and Helen Stuffins for the use of their encyclopaedic knowledge about food and growing, Norman Ireland and Jane Percy-Robb for editorial and culinary counsel, Tim Bates for the occasional but essential reality check, and Paul Nero for taking care of business while the book was being written. Finally I would like to thank my wife Fiona for creating a blissful household in which the writing of a book could happen smoothly; and my sons Finn and Fergus for being good little boys throughout.

Preface

I think it started with asparagus. Our short, splendid asparagus season should be marked in the diaries of all British gourmets. But even though I'm a keen cook and food enthusiast, with kitchen shelves straining under the weight of the latest glossy cookbooks, I didn't know when it was. In fact, beyond some general notions of spring lamb and game in the autumn, I realized that I didn't know anything much about food's seasons. Was this normal? A few conversations with equally food-crazed contemporaries suggested it was. It seemed that unless you were a farmer, grower, food expert or over sixty, your awareness of what's in season when was about as extensive as mine.

This struck me as a serious gap in our knowledge. Despite a renaissance in British home cooking, coupled with a rediscovery of local produce through farmers' markets and enthusiastic celebrity chefs, many of us are missing some important information. What's the use of a fancy gooseberry recipe in November?

Of course there are references – like the baffling monthly tables of vegetables that sometimes feature in food books – and plenty of seasonally orientated cookbooks, from landmarks like Margaret Costa's *Four Seasons Cookery Book* to the River Café books. But none of these offers an easily digestible answer to simple questions such as 'What's good now?' or 'Is lamb good now?' Nor do they go on to explore why it's good, the answers to which can be both interesting and useful.

I wanted to know what was good to cook and eat without having to plough through pages of recipes. The more I read and researched, the more I learned about the delightful cycle of seasonal food in Britain, and the more I realized that my dream reference book didn't exist.

So I had to write it. Asparagus, by the way, is on page 68.

Introduction

Life in Britain was once intimately entwined with the seasons. Our survival depended on a wealth of skills we developed to take advantage of the growing cycle and to deal with the barren winter. We learned when to plant and harvest to ensure fresh food was available for as long as possible. We knew exactly when wild foods were ready for the taking. And we learned to dry, salt, smoke, preserve and store food to keep us going through the lean times, or to take advantage of abundance. Our year turned to a cycle that was driven by the seasons, with the last autumn harvests heralding the end of the old year and the beginning of the new.

For many of us today, technology has reduced the seasons to little more than an aesthetic distraction. Heating and air-conditioning keep us comfortable all year round. Refrigeration, high-technology storage and a globalized food market mean that we can eat whatever we want, whenever we want. The year follows very different rhythms: the school year, the tax year, the financial year.

As a result, what awareness we have of food's seasons is diminishing rapidly. It has arguably been on the wane for hundreds of years, since a series of land enclosures starting in the 1500s began to reduce the amount of common land on which small farmers and labourers could grow food and raise livestock for themselves. By the late eighteenth century, when enclosures accelerated, many had been forced off the land and into towns and cities, where, according to food historian Colin Spencer, 'under the slavery of long hours and pittance wages, their diet declined to bread, jam, tea and sugar'. While we might think that junk food, far removed from nature's cycles, is a relatively recent phenomenon, it has in fact been a part of British life for hundreds of years.

As the first people to industrialize, Britons were the first to lose our connection with the land and the seasons. We regained it – albeit briefly, and under duress – in the Second World War, when the 'dig for victory' campaign had the whole nation growing its own food and in better health than at any other time in the twentieth century. After the war, though, the combination of agricultural subsidy and chemical farming severed this connection anew, and brought us to where we are today: a world of cheap, year-round abundance. So should we care about the relationship between food and the seasons when it is no longer a matter of life and death; when we (in Britain at least) can eat what we want, when we want?

I believe we should. For a start, there's the simple fact that food tastes better in season. From spring lamb to asparagus, from apples to wild salmon, fresh, local produce is better to eat than food that has been raised artificially, or that has travelled halfway around the world in a controlled-atmosphere container. There are straightforward reasons for this. Take tomatoes. They like to grow in rich, well-composted soil and need good strong sun to ripen properly. The flavour of a fine tomato is a result of the subtle interplay between nutritious soil and sunlight. So it should come as no surprise that 'fresh' tomatoes, planted in an artificial substrate and grown out of season in an air-conditioned greenhouse, taste of nothing much at all. Or take intensively farmed salmon, also available all year round. Fooled into growing by artificial light, drenched in chemicals, drugged up to the eyeballs and crammed into pens at densities of up to 20kg per cubic metre, they are not in good shape when they reach the supermarket. Wild fish, on the other hand, caught in season, have reached a prime condition that results from a natural life cycle and are an infinitely superior product.

Of course we can get many foods all year round. But it's a treat and a privilege to eat them in season, because for much of the year many foods are not at their best.

Then there's the question of how sustainable our approach to food production and consumption is. Our 'year-round abundance' has carried a heavy price. The problems of industrial agriculture – from unhappy salmon to battery hens to pesticide-soaked vegetables – are well documented and have provoked a surge in the sales of organic produce. This is to the good, because apart from giving us foods free from agrochemicals whose deleterious effects are thought to range from poorer child health to male infertility, organic production has many benefits. It promotes biodiversity and soil quality; it reduces the pollution of waterways and land. And most of the time it gives us food that is healthier, richer in nutrients and tastier.

But adherence to organic standards alone is not necessarily a sustainable way for us to produce food; nor does it guarantee a superior product. Flying in organic spring onions from Mexico and collecting them by car from a supermarket creates 300 times more CO_2 emissions than if they were grown locally and delivered by an organic box scheme. And they don't taste as good either.

In a world where man-made climate change is becoming an urgent issue, what we eat is more than just a matter of taste. Buying in season encourages us to buy locally, whether from the farmers' market in town or the specialist sheep farmer who sells direct. Supermarkets may pride themselves on an ever-growing range of organic produce, but if a kilo of apples has made the flight from New Zealand in March, are they really going to taste as good as a well-stored late British variety? If you accept that human activity contributes to climate change, are the New Zealand apples worth the kilo of CO_2 they will produce compared to the 50g if the same kilo were sourced locally? Despite the fact that we grow perhaps the best apples in the world, Britain has lost 60 per cent of its apple orchards since 1970, thanks in part to the bureaucratic madness that paid growers to dig them up. Buying locally and in season encourages local producers, who are building a more sustainable food industry, contributing to a renaissance in British produce and cuisine and creating a better environment.

Most of all, though, eating with the seasons brings a rich variety into our lives. Where's the fun in eating the same things all year round? By being closely aware of what's in season, you get twelve months' worth of gastronomic treats, and satisfying answers to the perpetual question of what to buy and cook for yourself, family and friends. Today, the nearest thing to a seasonal gastronomic event in Britain is the annual consumption of an oversized fowl accompanied by miniature cabbages, about both of whose qualities many have, at best, ambivalent feelings.

The seasons have much more to offer than this. British produce gives us a huge range of reasons to celebrate throughout the year. From the autumnal abundance of fruit, game and vegetables to the spring treats of lamb, fresh greens and mackerel, there is (almost) always something good, fresh and locally produced for us to enjoy.

However, unless we are enthusiasts, farmers, or live close to rural tradition, many of us have only a vestigial awareness of what's in season when. Regaining this knowledge is not easy. Chefs and food professionals tend to keep it to themselves, occasionally giving away tempting titbits in their recipes: 'And now, of course, is the perfect time to eat lobster!' Why? How do they know this? How do we get to know this stuff?

The purpose of this book is to put comprehensive knowledge of food's seasons back in the hands of people who buy food. It's not a recipe book – there are plenty of those already. *Seasonal Food* is a guidebook to what's in season when and why in Britain, so that you can eat produce at its best, contribute to a renaissance in local production, and simply revel in the variety of the seasons.

The seasons and their influence on food

Seasons start with the sun, the great fuel source that powers all of life on Earth. Its heat and light stimulate plants to grow and to convert its energy into food for themselves and the creatures that feed on them. Together with the seas, the land masses, the atmosphere and the planet's spin, the sun drives the weather systems that also determine where things can live and thrive.

But all of this highly complex interaction doesn't, on its own, give us the seasons. Our annual cycle of weather comes from two simple accidents of creation.

The first is that our planet's axis is gently tilted at a 23.5° angle. Without this, there would be no seasons in Britain, or perhaps seasons so extreme as to render the place uninhabitable. As it is, the angle of our annual procession around the sun means that its rays hit our hemisphere more directly for half the year, while for the rest of the time the southern half of the globe benefits. This gives us the annual variations in temperature and length of day to which our flora and fauna have had to adapt.

The second accident of creation is that we are fortunate enough to have a large, nearby moon that holds our axis reasonably steady in the face of gravitational assault from the sun and the planet Jupiter. Without the moon, which we also have to thank for tides and a host of other effects on natural systems, our 23.5° tilt (which still varies slightly over long periods of time) would swing wildly and give us chaotic, unpredictable, probably life-threatening weather.

So two happy cosmic accidents have conspired to give us a stable progression of seasons that have created the variety in nature's activity that we see in Britain today. But what are the seasons and when do they happen?

The answer is not as obvious as one might think. The *astronomical* seasons simply follow Earth's orbit, suggesting that winter and summer start at the solstices on 21 December and 21 June; and that spring and autumn begin at the equinoxes (21 March and 21 September). However, it is obvious to all of us that although they are the times of the strongest and weakest solar radiation, the summer and winter solstices do not represent the extremes of the seasons; nor are the equinoxes the depths of spring and autumn.

The main reason for this is something called 'heat lag'. Land heats up and cools down more slowly than air; and water more slowly still. So because land and sea are still heating up or cooling down after the solstices, the hottest and coldest days tend to be around a month later. And because Britain's climate is so strongly influenced by the sea, the lag can be even longer, with a two-week difference between inland and coastal locations. Boosted by the Gulf Stream, the Atlantic's winter warmth gives Devon and Cornwall mean temperatures in January that compare favourably with the French Riviera.

And if you thought there were four seasons, think again. Meteorologists prefer to talk of five separate seasons that are characterized not only by temperature but also by the different weather types that prevail at different times of the year. *Early winter* (rain, wind, storms) runs from late November to early February; *late winter* (less rain) from February to March; *spring and early summer* (lowest rainfall) from April to early June; *high summer* (warm southerly winds, lots of rain) from June to early September; and *autumn* (high pressure, mists) from September to late November.

The most obvious way in which these seasons affect food is in the growing cycle of plants. Below 6°C, plants are 'resting' and they can begin growing again only when the average temperature rises above this level. In Britain, this threshold is reached at different points depending on a combination of factors: how far south you are, how close to the Atlantic, and how high up. In practice, this has meant that the start of the growing season sweeps up the country from Cornwall in the south-west around 14 February, and then northwards and upwards until growth finally kicks off in the high ground of northern England and Scotland on 1 April. Climate change (of which more later) is starting to affect these dates.

If we want to see how the seasons are really organized in relation to food, however, a look back in time is instructive. Traditional pre-Christian Celtic festivals were tied both to the astronomical calendar, with four celebrations occurring at the solstices and equinoxes, and to the cycle of growth, with another four that related to significant moments in the life of the land. On 31 October Samhain, now known as Hallowe'en, marked the end of the last harvests and the beginning of a new annual cycle. Imbolc, which was held on 2 February, marked the reawakening of the land and was associated with lambing and the appearance of early flowers. Beltane, more commonly celebrated as May Day, was an earthy celebration of the blooming fertility that was all around in nature. And on 1 August, Lughnasadh or Lammas (the latter from Saxon words meaning 'loaf festival') marked the first harvests and a celebration of plenty.

The food chain, like the seasons, starts with the sun's energy. Plants convert it into carbohydrates, oils and proteins that enable them to grow and provide the food source on which all other creatures depend. The heat of the sun determines when this process starts, then acts as a 'volume control', with greater warmth creating a greater rate of plant development. The cold of winter also acts as a stimulant to growth, providing an 'on' switch for plants such as winter wheat, parsnips and sugar beet. The sun's light acts as a trigger for the growth of other plants that wait for a critical length of daylight before they come into flower.

Animals, birds, insects and fish set their calendars according to the seasonal larder, breeding, migrating or hibernating to take advantage of abundance or cope with shortages. In some cases they act as the servants of the plants. Flowers and blossoms, for example, are not colourful in order to please humans but rather to coerce insects into pollinating them and rendering them fertile. Fruit plays a similarly gentle trick, appealing to the appetites of creatures who unwittingly spread its seeds together with a healthy dollop of fertilizer. All of this has meant that many wild fauna have also developed a pronounced seasonality, raising young in the spring and fattening themselves for winter in the abundant autumn, at which time their more systematic predators (us) have the best chance of a seasonal meal.

Creatures that are now domesticated for farming and have no real seasonality, even if raised organically, were once eaten according to a seasonal rhythm. Unable to feed their cattle and pigs over the barren winter, our ancestors slaughtered all except those kept for breeding and labour at Martinmas (11 November) and set about preserving the meats. Two periods of fasting (Advent and Lent) were conveniently slotted into this hungry time. With the introduction of fodder crops such as turnips in the seventeenth and eighteenth centuries, livestock could be fed over the winter and therefore largely lost their seasonality.

Overall, though, the seasons have had an enormous influence on what we eat, not only in terms of when we can eat it but also in the skills and techniques we developed to ensure a healthy year-round diet. Salting, smoking, pickling, preserving and bottling were all developed largely to take advantage of seasonal abundance and lay down stores for the lean times. Today, our high-tech, globalized food market has rendered many of these techniques unnecessary. But without the seasons, we might not have smoked ham. What a loss that would be!

Will the seasons stay where they are? Even the most urbanized adult Briton cannot have failed to notice that things are getting warmer. The Central England Temperature series – the longest available instrumental record of temperature in the world – shows average temperatures in Britain dating back to 1659. It reveals a gradual warming trend starting from the time of mid-nineteenth century industrialization, then a sharp upward trend through the 1990s, the warmest decade on record.

By 2050, UK temperatures are predicted to rise by somewhere between 0.9°C and 2.4°C. Because of the climate's complexity, it is difficult to predict exactly how such warming will affect our seasons. For example, a 1.5°C rise in temperature is the equivalent of moving south 200–300km or losing 200m of height. In theory, this would mean growing crops in the north of England that are currently grown mainly in the south, such as maize and sweetcorn. This change can already be seen in agriculture: from 1985 to 1999, the area of vineyards cultivated in the UK more than doubled. We will have a longer growing season (running from 28 January to 22 December, the year 2000's was the longest on record), with a year-round growing season not far away. But we may have drier summers and wetter winters, which will influence what can be grown. And if, as some suggest, melting icecaps slow or stop the Gulf Stream, then, ironically, global warming will give Britain a more continental climate, with severe winters and shorter, hotter summers.

So the seasons are changing. But then they always were. Whatever happens to the climate, as long as the planet stays at its 23.5° angle, we in Britain will still have an annual variation in what can be grown, raised and eaten locally. Keeping track of this, in order to eat food that is both at its best and produced sustainably, will always be worth the effort.

Favourite foods from shortage and glut

Living by seasonal produce alone would be tough. It's something that only a true hunter-gatherer could lay claim to doing, and it is many thousands of years since such a lifestyle prevailed in Britain. We've used agriculture to 'cheat' the seasons for a long time now, growing surpluses that can be stored to provide staples through the lean months, or herding animals to ensure a constant food source. In recent years, of course, we have also used technology to cheat the seasons: canning, freezing, irradiating and air-freighting food to ensure an uninterrupted, year-round supply.

Our ancestors did not have access to such preserving techniques; nor, for a long time, did they understand the biological processes that cause food to spoil. It was probably by trial, error and happy accident that 'traditional' methods of preserving food, such as pickling, salting, smoking, drying and sealing were discovered. These practices did not arise solely because of seasonal variation in supply. The religious observance of meat-free days, for example, drove a demand for salted and dried cod. Potting, which involves cooking food then sealing it in a container, also helped to protect foods when they were transported. Pickled cabbage – commonly known as sauerkraut – was famously a protection against scurvy on long sea voyages because the preserving process retains the vegetable's vitamin C content. Captain Cook took 19,000lb of sauerkraut on his voyages and lost not a single man to the disease.

What distinguishes these traditional preserving techniques from their modern descendants, however, is that they change the taste of the food that is being preserved, often for the better. In some cases, they create food that has become of enormous significance for different societies. Salt cod, for example, is little more than a curiosity for most British people, but the Portuguese hold it in high esteem. Pickled cabbage is an important dish for Germans, Koreans and French from the Alsace region; but many elsewhere find the idea decidedly unpleasant (yet often change their minds after a taste). The Swedes are unique in their passion for fermented herring, whose powerful smell is famous for repelling all other nationalities. Buried, rotted shark is treasured in

Iceland. And, astonishing though it may seem to those for whom it is an integral part of their national identity, much of the world is ignorant of the pleasures of bacon, perhaps the finest preserved food of all.

Preserving has therefore created iconic foods; and the need to preserve has, at least in part, arisen from the effect of the seasons on the supply of food. Driven by the challenge of maintaining a nutritious and interesting diet throughout the year, our forebears created foods that remain central to the way we eat today, even if their origin is long forgotten.

The seasonal pig

Bacon has no seasonality today; nor indeed do any of the products of the British pig, except for the smallholder or specialist breeder. Yet pigs used to be a crucial part of the annual cycle in Britain, with bacon the longest-lasting and therefore most treasured product of the beast. Pigs had an incredibly useful role in the peasant economy. Even more omnivorous than humans, pigs convert almost any food, and food waste, into fine meat and high-quality manure. Traditionally, they were fattened through the year and killed in the autumn to provide a supply of protein, flavour and fat through the winter. (Although fat today seems something either to be avoided or embraced completely, depending on one's fad diet of choice, to our peasant forebears it was an essential ingredient to provide energy to combat the rigours of the leaner months.) Before slaughter, the pigs' diet – and their quality – was improved by a final feast of windfall apples, acorns and beech mast; pigs are woodland creatures at heart. But as Dorothy Hartley points out in *Food in England*, they could provide much more than just food for the winter: 'A pig killed in November would still provide fresh meat and brawn and pie till Christmas, and ham, bacon and lardie cakes for an entire year.'

Pig meat may indeed be valuable, but it spoils easily, so quick work and careful techniques are required to get the most out of it. The blood, guts and offal were dealt with first, creating delicacies such as black puddings, sausages, chitterlings (cooked intestines) and faggots, all of which helped to eke out for a few weeks the bits of the pig that would otherwise go off too quickly. Other parts, in particular the sides and haunches, were preserved by salting (and maybe smoked as well) to keep for much longer as ham and bacon. The latter, in a large piece or 'flitch', would be hung from the ceiling or high in the fireplace: smoke acts as a deterrent to insects, forms an antiseptic seal on the meat's surface and, of course, imparts an extra note to the flavour. For poor families in rural Ireland, bacon was such a luxury that it gave rise to a dish jokingly called 'potatoes and point', whereby the potato was merely pointed at the priceless bacon in the hope that it might take on some of its flavour.

The presence of a side of bacon excited particular passion in the mightily passionate William Cobbett, whose *Cottage Economy* of 1821 was an attempt to give back to the labouring classes the skills in self-sufficiency that the industrial revolution had taken from them. He saw a flitch of bacon – providing alluring, wholesome food and flavour through hard winter months – as a much better guarantor of domestic and social harmony than any amount of religious observance. Cobbett's passion was driven by the depredations of both industrialization and land enclosures. In drastically reducing the amount of common land on which animals could be grazed and run, enclosures eventually made it difficult for poor rural families to keep livestock for their own use; and legislation aimed at urban rather than rural hygiene made it harder still. By 1750, a few thousand landowners owned much of the land in Britain. Together with industrialization, the social changes wrought by this upheaval are seen as largely responsible for the decline of peasant cuisine in Britain, to the point where today we revere the earthy rural cuisines of France and Italy in preference to our own.

We didn't forget bacon, though. It's no longer a seasonal food, for which we should be thankful; but we have the seasons to thank for the salting and smoking that brought it to us. The contemporary bacon buyer should choose carefully. Of all the foods for which it is worth paying a premium to ensure a wholesome product that is the result of good husbandry, bacon should be at the top of the list. Much bacon is cured in an industrialized process in which the meat is injected with brine and preservatives, creating a waterlogged and inferior product. And the taste of 'smoked' bacon sometimes comes from 'liquid smoke', an artificial flavouring also used, for example, to flavour crisps. Most significantly, industrial-scale pig production is extremely cruel, for pigs are intelligent and social creatures. It is also environmentally disastrous: a single US pig 'factory' can produce as much waste matter as the people of New York City.

Buying bacon that has been dry-cured, or otherwise traditionally produced, means happier pigs and a much better breakfast. On that lighter note, we should also be grateful to the seasons for all the related porky delicacies that still play a part in our cuisine: from magnificent, succulent hams all the way down to the humble pork scratching, originally just another product of our efforts to make use of everything in the pig except the 'oink'. Today, there is a renewed interest in the pig-as-seasonal-delicacy. American chef Anthony Bourdain has written lyrically of his participation in a traditional Portuguese pig-killing. In *A Cook's Tour*, he describes how the rigours of the slaughter are relieved (for all except the pig) by the celebration of gastronomy and tradition that follows immediately after. And in his *River Cottage Cookbook* gastro-smallholder Hugh Fearnley-Whittingstall makes a seductive case for the merits of keeping a pair of pigs – at least until the autumn.

Big strong pies

It may be stretching the point a little, but we could partially thank the seasons for another great British delicacy, and a pork-related one: pies. Why pies? Because their origin too lies in preservation. Cooking is one way of helping to preserve food, as the heat destroys the enzymes that speed the process of decay. Sealing cooked food stops the oxygen in the air from turning fats rancid, and also keeps out bugs; so cooked, sealed food is likely to stay edible for a while longer than raw food. An early way of achieving this seal was with pastry: medieval pies had a crust made of coarse flour which was thrown to the dogs or given to servants rather than being eaten by the householder. Pies were also made to keep food fresh in transit; their thick, sturdy crusts could store plenty of valuable produce: lampreys, geese, whatever. In *English Food*, Jane Grigson cites a startling 'Yorkshire Christmas Pye' recipe from eighteenth- century writer Hannah Glasse that contains a turkey, a goose, a fowl, a partridge and a pigeon and, terrifyingly, a bushel of flour. Pies were packed in special leather cases to help them withstand the buffeting of a journey by stagecoach. The introduction of a liquid filling that would eventually set to a jelly (as in a contemporary pork pie) created a complete airtight seal that gave the pie better longevity.

More efficient preserving and transportation techniques mean that the monster travelling pie is sadly no longer with us. Only the Denby Dale pie, produced about once a generation and whose last exemplar, in 2000, weighed 9.03 tonnes, still attains truly spectacular proportions. But its many smaller relatives remain another popular peculiarity of British cuisine, at least part of whose origin is in the seasons.

Preserving fleeting fruits

Anyone who has been moderately successful at fruit or vegetable gardening, or passed a bramble patch bursting with ripe fruit, has been faced with the same question: what to do with all the excess? Root vegetables and tubers such as carrots and potatoes lend themselves to storage, assuming one can create the necessary cool, dark conditions. Other fruit and vegetables can be dried and kept for long periods: for example, peas, garlic, onions, apples. But the softer, more delicate fruit and veg need to be 'processed' if one is to enjoy anything more than a fleeting annual acquaintance with them.

Sharing Cobbett's passion and his critique of many aspects of modernity is John Seymour, whose 1975 classic *The Complete Book of Self-sufficiency* is still going strong. Seymour's bête noire is the deep freeze: 'The urge to prolong unnaturally the season of every mortal thing, by embalming them in deep-freezes and the like, should be resis-ted.' Yet, as he points out, if the 'self-supporter' is to enjoy a bit of flavour and variety after the harvest months, preserving things is a necessity. For the simple reason that they change foods for the better, Cobbett recommends traditional methods. Few of us are self-sufficient today, so we're not compelled to go into a frenzy of bottling, drying, pickling and jam-making each autumn, but the legacy of this once common annual activity is a further treasury of great things to eat whose origin is in the turn of the seasons. If the freezer had been with us from the start, we might never have experienced pickles or jam.

For some produce, though, freshness is so key to the experience that to preserve would somehow be pointless: one thinks (again) of asparagus. In this case, the short season is part of the fun. For other things, in particular the berry fruits that grow so well in our climate yet whose season is so brief, preserving has brought us foods that are memorable in their own right, from jams, jellies and pickles to fruit wines. In *The Shepherd's Calendar*, extracts from which introduce each month in this book, the poet John Clare talks of the promise of elderberry wine:

Here the industrious huswives wend their way
Pulling the brittle branches carefull down
And hawking loads of berrys to the town
Wi' unpretending skill yet half divine
To press and make their eldern berry wine
That bottl'd up becomes a rousing charm
To kindle winter's icy bosom warm.

We may not have particularly icy winters any more, but it's still worth going to the trouble of making elderberry wine or jelly, or any preserves or home-made wines, for that matter. When we save the essence of something ephemeral, it provides us with yet another delicacy whose origin is in the seasons.

One could create an endless list of such foods. Bacon, pies, jams, pickles and wine are a small, highly personal sample. Yet they illustrate how, in forcing our forebears to be inventive in order to survive and enjoy an interesting diet, the annual cycle of weather in Britain has left us with a great deal more than just a fascinating annual variety of fresh edible produce.

Using this book

Although *Seasonal Food* contains a few recipes and some hints on cooking and preparation, it is a guidebook rather than a cookbook. The premise of the book is that the best eating starts with the best ingredients, and the best ingredients are local, in-season produce. By setting out what is in season when and why, it will help you to eat food that is at its best, whether you are buying it and cooking it yourself or ordering it in a restaurant.

The few recipes in this book are mostly simple ones that celebrate the quality of the produce on which they are based. There are many, many cookbooks available with more creative recipes for seasonal produce, and the bibliography (*p. 157*) contains a selection of some of the best.

Seasonal Food is not prescriptive: it doesn't suggest that we turn back the clock and throw ourselves on the mercy of the seasons, as our distant ancestors had to. We've long since dealt with the problem of seasonal hardship. Well before refrigeration and air-freighting, we were able to guarantee year-round food supplies and variety with, for example, preservation and storage techniques, or the use of fodder crops to keep a meat supply going through the winter. If the book prescribes anything, it is that we rediscover the astonishing variety of seasonal food beyond just turkey and sprouts.

Finally, *Seasonal Food* covers only British produce. This is not for reasons of nationalism, nor is it a rejection of the international trade in food: life without such favourites as marmalade, Parmesan cheese, coffee, good red wine or bananas would be diminished indeed. However, many things that grow perfectly in their British season are now supplied all year round, for example, strawberries, asparagus and apples. This book argues that often our own produce is best, and it questions the ecological and gastronomic wisdom of treating, storing and transporting food so that we can eat it at the 'wrong' time of year, particularly when, in some cases (such as apples), we could eat our own, superior produce for a much longer season if the food chain were arranged for the good of consumers rather than large corporations.

The most important reason for this book's focus on British produce is the simple one that it is excellent. Our country's poor gastronomic reputation comes not from the fact that we can't grow or raise good things. We can. Rather, it stems from complex, interrelated historical factors such as our early concentration of land ownership in few hands, early industrialization and the impact of the twentieth century's great wars, as well as a pervasive 'science knows best' attitude. Then the cult of Mediterranean food – a sun-drenched alternative to post-war drabness – knocked British food traditions back even further.

Today, the excellence of British produce, from fruit and veg to cheese and meat, is being rediscovered, as are some of our gastronomic traditions. Eating locally and in season will help accelerate this rediscovery and set us on a path to a tastier, healthier and more sustainable food chain.

Notes on the tables

The introductory tables for each month concentrate on the seasonal treats that feature in the text, as well as highlighting what's coming into season and what's going out. These tables do not list all the produce that is in season in a particular month; that would create too much repetition. If you need an at-a-glance view of everything that is in season in each month, there is a comprehensive master table on pages 152–5. This also contains information such as whether food is fresh or from store, and whether (and in which month) it is featured in the book.

The seasons listed for fruit and vegetables in this table – and throughout the book – use an average for Britain. Depending on how far north or south you live, produce may appear up to a month later or earlier than listed. With the exception of 'forced' produce (such as rhubarb, chicory and seakale), all the seasons listed for fruit and vegetables refer to produce that matures outdoors without artificial heat or shelter.

I have chosen not to include produce that is available all year round, or that has no relevant, interesting or easily defined British seasonality: for example, beef, pork, chicken, spinach, lettuce, eggs, many cheeses and many fish species.

Seasonal food festivals in Britain

MONTH	EVENT	WHAT, WHERE AND WHEN
January	Wassailing Wakefield Festival of Rhubarb	Exhorting the apple trees to fruit, apple-growing areas, 17 Jan Celebrating forced rhubarb, Wakefield, end Jan–early Feb
February	Potato Day	Celebrating potato diversity, Ryton Organic Gardens, Coventry, early Feb
March	Blossom Trail	Follow plum, damson and apple blossom, Evesham, Worcester, March
April	Dock Pudding Competition Damson Day	Who's made the best dock pudding? Mytholmroyd, W. Yorks, April A celebration of damsons to coincide with the blossom, Lyth Valley, weekend before Easter
May	Silver Band Asparagus Auction Cheese Rolling	Raising money with asparagus, Fleece Inn, Bretforton, Worcs, late May Rolling cheese down hills, various Gloucestershire locations, May
June	British Strawberry Day Cherry Pie Fair	Events around the country promoting summer fruits, mid-June Local fair, Seer Green, Bucks, around 22 June

MONTH	EVENT	WHAT, WHERE AND WHEN
July	Soft Fruit Event Oyster Festival	Gooseberries & more, Roger Plant Centre, Pickering, N. Yorks, mid-July Outside the British season, but with fun events nonetheless, Whitstable, Kent, July
August	Lammas Fair Plum Day Faversham Hop Festival Isle of Wight Garlic Festival Gooseberry Show Opening of the Oyster Fisheries	Harvest events, most notable in Ballycastle, Antrim, late Aug A celebration of plums, Pershore, Worcestershire, end Aug Celebrating the hop harvest, Faversham, Kent, end Aug Enjoying the garlic harvest, Newchurch, Isle of Wight, 3rd week Aug Who's got the biggest gooseberry? Egton Bridge, N. Yorks, early Aug The mayor eats the season's first native oyster, Colchester, Essex, Aug
September	Crabapple Fair Pear Day Abergavenny Food Festival Ludlow Marches Food Festival British Food Fortnight	Also includes gurning championship, Egremont, Cumbria, 3rd Sat in Sept Pear-related fun, Cawthorn, near Barnsley, S. Yorks, end Sept Celebrating local & regional food, Abergavenny, Monmouthshire, mid-Sept Famous for its 'sausage trail', Ludlow, Shropshire, mid-Sept Drawing attention to regional food & drink, nationwide, mid-Sept to early Oct
October	Apple Day Falmouth Oyster Festival National Quince Day	Major apple celebration, events nationwide, 21 October Celebrates this traditional oyster fishery, Falmouth, Cornwall, mid-Oct Touring the quince trees, Norton Priory, Runcorn, Cheshire, early Oct
November	Buy Nothing Day British Sprout Festival	A good excuse to eat your own produce, international, end Nov All things to do with sprouts, Chipping Campden, Glos, end Oct–early Nov
December	Yule/Solstice/ Christmas/Hogmanay	Time for your own food festival, everywhere, 21–31 December

January

Treats for the month

January	Seasonal Treats	Coming in	Going out
Vegetables	Kale Kohlrabi Leeks Swede	Broccoli, sprouting	
Fruit & Nuts		Rhubarb, forced	
Meat, Game & Poultry	Hare Venison		Goose Snipe Woodcock
Fish & Seafood			

January

'Withering and keen the winter comes
While comfort flyes to close shut rooms'

Cold, wet, mist, snow, fog. All this, and the holiday season has just ended. In addition, many are struggling with the self-denial of new year's resolutions. Following on from the untrammelled gluttony of Christmas, January is not a month that we associate with seasonal gastronomic celebration. But celebrate it we must, casting resolutions to the biting wind, for there is much that is good to eat. And the coldest month of the year is definitely not a time for a low-calorie diet.

Now is a good moment to renew (or begin) an acquaintance with hare, a rare but wonderful seasonal treat that will feed many, or make many different dishes. Venison, which in one form or another is in season for much of the year, also has a hearty richness that suits the season. To accompany these, there is little that is fresh, with many fruit and vegetables now coming from store. However, the hardiest plants – such as kale, leeks and swede – are still fresh in the ground, untroubled by the vile weather and ready to make warming meals.

With much of nature shut down for the winter, this is a time to encourage it to wake up again: the tradition of 'wassailing' orchards, in ceremonies that exhort them to be fruitful in the coming year, still takes place in apple-growing areas on 17 January. And at the end of the month, there are events to mark the arrival of forced rhubarb, which promises a flash of colour and freshness in a dark season.

Hare

Such a noble, graceful creature; it almost seems a shame to eat hare. But it makes for such a fine and copious feast that hare is one of the best seasonal delights available. Brown hare – the type commonly found in England – does not have a formal 'closed' season, but it cannot be sold from March to July, which gives it some peace in its breeding season. The smaller mountain hare, which prefers Scotland and also pops up in Derbyshire's Peak District, has a similar season, but formally enforced. The Game Conservancy Trust also advises against shooting brown hare in February, as this can remove much of the breeding stock. Like much wild game, therefore, hare is a meal for the autumn and winter.

A hare is a much more substantial meal than a rabbit: one animal can feed up to eight people or make a series of delicious meals. It is also richer and more gamey in flavour, and needs to be hung for a few days for its flavour to develop. It is widely available in good butchers and game dealers, but the hare population has declined by 75 per cent since the Second World War, with contemporary numbers estimated at 800,000. The reason for this is not hunting, which accounts for less than 5 per cent, but modern farming techniques. A brown hare's favourite habitat is a traditional arable farm, where it can munch on the crops and hide in the grass of 'leys', fields left fallow. Modern farms don't have the cover that hares need, and their crop rotations leave insufficient food for the creatures throughout the year. Hares are thus vulnerable to hunger; but mainly to foxes, who prey on their young. So restoring hare populations is another of the many, many reasons for moving away from highly industrialized agriculture. And eating hare is another vote for their conservation in the wild, for hare could never be intensively farmed.

Preparing hare is a matter of nerve: even the most pragmatic cooks discuss the job of skinning and gutting in grim terms. Probably best to ask the butcher to do the job. Adding to the gore of hare cuisine are the facts that the blood thickens and flavours the stews in which the creatures are often cooked; and that the head makes great gravy. Still, none of this should deter the hare gourmet. One hare can make several dishes: a roast of the shoulder and saddle, a stew of the legs; and a soup from the head and trimmings. The classic 'jugged' hare, which uses the blood and offal to achieve its rich texture and flavour, is one of the finest of stews. Traditionally cooked in a tall earthenware jug set in a large pan of water, it can be made in a good casserole dish by those of us without period kitchen equipment.

Kale

Kale is tough. Not in a way that makes it difficult to eat, for it is a very fine brassica. It is tough because of its ability to grow in – and stand up to – the most rigorous weather that the British Isles can throw at it. It thrives in winter, when it can provide a source of fresh greenery all the way from September through till March. And it grows well in cold, wet places, which is why it became famous as a staple of Scottish crofters in the days before the Highland clearances. The 'kale yard' or 'kailyard' was a feature of crofters' dwellings and even gave its name to a nineteenth-century school of writers sometimes accused of sentimentalizing the country's past.

Kale also has an ability to keep going when almost everything else that is fresh and green has been decimated by winter: there is even a variety called Hungry Gap. John Seymour commends kale to the smallholder: 'Leave kale until you really need it: after the Brussels sprouts have rotted, the cabbage are finished, the slugs have had the rest of the celery, and the ground is two feet deep in snow and only your kale plants stand above it like ship-wrecked schooners.' So kale is a good thing to have in the garden, a guaranteed fresh green vegetable at a time when little else is in season. If you are growing your own, kale leaves can be picked off the plant when you want them, making it even more practical as a winter staple.

Despite its austere image, kale has become surprisingly fashionable of late. Black kale, or cavolo nero, has the added advantage of looking good – with long, dark, blue-green leaves shaped like the funeral plumes of horses – as well as a glamorous Italian name. Like all kale, its taste develops after a good frost, another reason for its position as a seasonal treat for the depths of winter.

Kale is cooked like any cabbage, although its tough stalks need to be removed. It can be lightly steamed and served on its own to accompany something hearty like a good fat sausage or two; or it works well in sturdy soups such as the Tuscan classic *Ribollita*, a trendy home for a now fashionable vegetable.

Kohlrabi

A small, bald sphere with sparse, protruding stems, kohlrabi would look more at home in orbit than in your kitchen. It is, however, a pretty down-to-earth vegetable, related to turnip and swede (*see pp. 84 and 33*) and with a similarly unglamorous alternative use as animal fodder. Kohlrabi is tasty, though, and it's popular in Germany and central Europe. Its exotic name is a combination of the German word for kale and turnip's species name, *rapa*. Unlike turnip and swede, kohlrabi's smooth swollen stem-base (it is not a root) grows above ground, making a row of the ready-to-harvest plants look weirdly ornamental. Like its relatives, kohlrabi stores energy in the summer so that it can lie dormant in the winter and flower in the spring.

Although it can be harvested from the summer onwards – for it is quick to mature – kohlrabi, like many brassicas, is also a useful winter vegetable. Its culinary uses suit both seasons. Kohlrabi can be eaten raw: grated, or sliced micro-thin and added to salads, where its cabbage/turnip/cauliflower flavour adds interest. For wintry dishes, kohlrabi can be braised, roasted, or added to soups and stews. It is at its best when about the size of a tennis ball, no bigger; and should always be peeled. The stalks and leaves, if any are left, can be eaten like cabbage.

Leeks

What a magnificent thing is a leek. At a time of year when there's little else happen-
ing in the kitchen garden, leeks sit patiently in the ground, whatever the weather, waiting for you to dig them up and make lovely things out of them. So while leeks have a
long season, being available fresh from August until March, they come into their own
in the depths of winter, when fresh seasonal vegetables are in short supply. The stock
of the leek has risen and fallen over the ages. Alan Davidson notes in the *Oxford
Companion to Food* that the Romans esteemed their fine flavour over onions and
garlic, which were seen as food fit only for the poor. In more recent times, though,
leeks have also been associated with the mush of overboiled institutional cooking, as
well as with the macho competitive vegetable growing of northern England, in which
size matters much more than eating quality.

Today, the leek has been rediscovered for the gourmet vegetable it truly is. Its
subtle flavour, lacking the bite of its relatives onion and garlic, means it is a fine dish
in its own right (simply steamed, sautéd or even grilled) as well as making it a good
flavouring for soups and stocks. It is the basis of at least two famous soups, Vichyssoise
and Cock-a-leekie. Leeks are also easy to grow, thriving in cold, wet conditions that
deter other edible plants.

The stem of a leek is blanched white because it has been earthed up beneath the soil;
while this is typically the bit that is eaten, the green leaves are useful too to flavour
stocks, so bear this in mind before you sling them on the compost.

In the midst of hymning their usefulness, *Complete Book of Self-sufficiency* author
John Seymour comments on leeks in magnificently grumpy style: 'The Welsh are very
sensible to have this excellent plant as an emblem and not some silly inedible flower
or a damned thistle.' Quite.

Leek risotto

This is a tasty, creamy, warming risotto and a fine home for your leeks.

4 leeks
generous splash of olive oil
2 litres/4 pints stock – chicken,
or vegetable will do
500g/1lb risotto rice

splash of dry vermouth or white wine
knob of butter
handful of freshly grated Parmesan
salt and freshly ground pepper

Chop the leeks finely from below where the leaves fan out. Heat the olive oil
in a heavy-bottomed pan and cook the leeks very gently until soft. While they
are cooking, heat up the stock to a low simmer in a saucepan.

When the leeks are soft, crank up the heat, tip in the rice, stir it so the
oil coats the grains and then add a liberal splash of dry vermouth or white
wine. Stir until the wine is absorbed, then lower the heat. Add the stock to the
rice, a ladleful at a time; stir constantly until each ladleful is absorbed before
adding another. When the risotto has absorbed the stock (after about 20 min-

utes) it should have reached a sticky consistency and the rice should have a residual chalky 'bite' but not be too hard. Add more stock if necessary, or hot water if you've run out. You can add some extra leek, diced thick and steamed, at this point to make it look nicer and add extra leeky flavour.

Stir in a generous knob of butter and a big handful of freshly grated Parmesan cheese, season to taste, and serve with more Parmesan on top. *Makes four generous portions.*

Swede

Like turnips (*see p. 84*), swedes lack glamour; although their American name, rutabaga, gives them a certain rough mystique. But they more than make up for this general dowdiness in taste and usefulness. Swede is thought to originate from a cross between a turnip and a cabbage, and a variant without the swollen edible stem-base is also grown as oilseed rape, a major (and highly visible) crop in Britain. Hardier than turnip, swede is an autumn/winter crop. It can stay in the ground until the end of the year and be stored thereafter, making it a reliable staple of the cold months.

Its toughness is a key reason for swede's popularity in Scotland, where it grows well, and it is the traditional Burns Night accompaniment to haggis alongside 'champit tatties' or mashed potatoes. 'Bashed neeps' are nothing to do with turnips; rather they are swede which has been peeled, chopped, boiled until tender and mashed with plenty of butter and pepper. Mashed swede (to give it its more effete English name) has a strong, sweet flavour and its taste and texture are the perfect partner for haggis or, if your stomach doesn't stretch to Scotland's national dish, sausages. Swede is good mashed together with carrots, or with potato to make an Orkney dish called clapshot. Its sugar content also makes it a good candidate for crisp, caramelized roasting alongside other favourites like parsnips and carrots.

Venison

Venison can be farmed, freezes well and is available all year. It is seasonal though, and this seasonality is mightily confusing because it varies according to the sex, location and species of the beast. The handy table on p. 35 illustrates the open shooting seasons for deer: looking at this table and thinking about venison's qualities, the cold of January seems a good time to seek it out.

The word 'venison' shares with 'beef', 'pork' and 'mutton' a derivation from the French and Latin, while the names of the creatures themselves are largely Old English-derived; this indicates, it is often said, that the posh people ate the meat while the peasants raised it. This has certainly been true of venison for a good few centuries. Deer parks were created by aristocrats to provide a source of both food and sport, to the chagrin of poorer people who were thus deprived of land to farm and live on. Such enclosures of land, not just for deer 'farming', have been a defining feature of Britain's food history.

Venison itself has an interesting lexicon. A deer that has just been shot must be 'gralloched' (eviscerated) immediately. Never has a word so graphically brought to mind the process it describes. And deer are also responsible for the phrase 'humble pie', from the word 'umbles', which describes the creature's offal, occasionally handed down to the grudging peasantry by their landlords. In *Food in England*, Dorothy Hartley seems delicately to speculate, via alternative terms such as 'dowsets' and 'stones', that 'umbles' refers specifically to the deer's testicles (suggested, incidentally, as a dish for the ladies in the Elizabethan play *Two Noble Kinsmen*).

Today, although the liver and kidneys can be used, the focus is on the venison itself, much more widely available than in previous centuries. Apart from the complexity of species, sex and season, the venison purchaser also has the deer's provenance to consider. Venison is either farmed, 'park' (managed on large country estates), or wild. Some rate farmed deer for its quality; and unlike for many four-legged creatures, welfare standards in this area of agriculture are high. Wild deer, which is shot for sport, often as part of culling programmes designed to manage the populations, is also rated. The mighty stags of Victorian paintings do not, however, make the best eating, and were presumably prized more for the decorative value of their severed heads and the machismo of their dispatch than for their meat.

Venison is rich and gamey, with a tendency to dryness. Most prized is the haunch, which makes a superb rare roast: a traditional wrapping to conserve moisture was the skin of a ham. Piquant accompaniments, particularly Cumberland sauce, are recommended. Tougher cuts make for good stews: venison braised with fat bacon and browned onions and made the day before it is to be eaten (*see below*) is a luxurious dish.

Braised venison

This takes some work, and should be made well in advance, for it demands overnight marinating followed by slow, attentive cooking; and its flavour improves with time. It is, however, a truly magnificent dish.

1.5kg/3lb haunch of venison	24 button onions, peeled
half bottle good red wine	large knob of butter
3 onions, chopped	a sprinkle of sugar
splash of brandy	24 button mushrooms, cleaned
olive oil	1 carrot, chopped
250g/$\frac{1}{2}$lb streaky bacon in one piece	3 cloves garlic, chopped
1 bayleaf	2 tablespoons plain flour
sprig of thyme	1 clove
	salt and freshly ground black pepper

Chop the venison into 5cm/2in cubes. Put it in a bowl and cover with the wine, the chopped onions, brandy, a splash of olive oil and copious grindings of black pepper. Cover and refrigerate overnight.

Then, well before you start cooking, drain the meat through a colander and collect the marinade for as long as possible. Dice the bacon. Tie up the bayleaf and thyme. Now you can begin cooking.

Heat a thin film of oil in a big, heavy-bottomed pan and fry the drained venison/onion mixture in batches, transferring it to a bowl when done, until it is all richly browned. In a separate pan, fry the button onions in a little of the butter and a sprinkle of sugar until deep brown, then the mushrooms (omitting the sugar).

Moving back to the meat pot, fry the chopped carrot, garlic and bacon in more butter until soft and dark, then stir in the flour, lower the heat, and stir until all is dark again. Add the marinade, a little at a time, scraping up residues on the bottom of the pan, then add the meat, herbs and clove; and the mushrooms and onions. Add more wine if needed. Season, bring to the boil, then cover and cook on a very low heat for at least two hours. Serve with celeriac and potato mash.

Serves six.

Open seasons for deer

	J	F	M	A	M	J	J	A	S	O	N	D
Red Stags (England)	•	•	•	•				•	•	•	•	•
Red Stags (Scotland)							•	•	•	•		
Red Hinds (England)	•	•									•	•
Red Hinds (Scotland)	•	•								•	•	•
Fallow Bucks (England)	•	•	•	•				•	•	•	•	•
Fallow Bucks (Scotland)	•	•	•	•				•	•	•	•	•
Fallow Does (England)	•	•									•	•
Fallow Does (Scotland)	•	•								•	•	•
Roe Bucks (England)				•	•	•	•	•	•	•		
Roe Bucks (Scotland)				•	•	•	•	•	•	•		
Roe Does (England)	•	•									•	•
Roe Does (Scotland)	•	•	•							•	•	•
Sika Stags (England)	•	•	•	•				•	•	•	•	•
Sika Stags (Scotland)							•	•	•	•		
Sika Hinds (England)	•	•									•	•
Sika Hinds (Scotland)	•	•								•	•	•

Source: *British Association for Shooting and Conservation*

• England • Scotland

February

Treats for the month

February	Seasonal Treats	Coming in	Going out
Vegetables	Cabbage, savoy Carrots Chicory and endive Onions		Salsify and scorzonera
Fruit & Nuts	Rhubarb, forced		
Meat, Game & Poultry	Rabbit		Hare Mallard Partridge Pheasant
Fish & Seafood			

February

'The sun peeps thro' the window pane
Which childern mark wi' laughing eye'

February is often a cold and harsh month, with unforgiving weather. Yet it can also contain hints of spring: traditionally, it was seen as a time when the land is reawakening from the deep sleep of winter. The pagan festival of Imbolc (adopted by Christians as Candlemas) celebrated this return to life: the name of the festival is thought to be derived from words meaning 'ewe's milk', which flows again at this time of year. Lambs born around now will be weaned in time for when the spring grass has its highest food value, in April and May. Although trees and plants are generally still dormant, there are signs of life: primroses and snowdrops are flowering now, and songthrushes start to make their voices heard. Fields tend to be bare, and much livestock is still kept indoors.

Despite February's barrenness, there is a great deal on offer for seasonal gourmets. Hardy brassicas like kale and savoy cabbage are still standing proud, and roots and potatoes from store are going strong: it's a time for comforting, warming dishes. The season for most wild game is all but over, with venison and maybe the odd rabbit still on the menu: it's best to leave the less prolific hare undisturbed. Seekers after something fresh and fruity have one major pleasure to look forward to at this time of year: delicate, pink forced rhubarb from Yorkshire (or from beneath your own forcing pots) is ready now.

Cabbage, savoy

A good savoy cabbage is about as far away from the overboiled mush of British cabbage legend as it is possible to get. Savoys have a pleasingly nutty flavour and an attractive texture, as long as they are not overcooked. Cabbages, of one sort or another, are available throughout the year (*see also spring greens, p. 63, red cabbage, p.147 and the cabbage seasonality table, p. 63*). Yet it is hard to get excited about pointy summer cabbages when there is so much else around, or about hard white winter cabbages when there is an abundance of tasty root vegetables fighting for our attention. Savoys deserve a special mention, though. Like kale (*see p. 30*) they are particularly hardy plants, best after the first frosts and able to stay in the ground through the winter, providing fresh green nutrition when it's most needed. So in February, when the suicide rate is at its highest, savoys are there to cheer you up.

Unlike many more humdrum cabbage varieties, savoys are esteemed for their gourmet qualities. Their strong, wrinkly leaves are ideal for the warming comfort food that is stuffed cabbage. If, however, life seems too short to stuff a cabbage, savoys are the easiest thing to cook well. First remove the tough central stalk, then all it takes is some rough chopping and a few minutes' steaming before the leaves can be served tossed in butter and freshly ground black pepper. The leaves also have a pleasing habit of picking up sauce in their dimples, making them tastier still. Savoy cabbage is the perfect partner for warming roasts, and leftovers make one half of a superior bubble and squeak.

Carrots

Carrots really have two seasons. The first is when the early spring carrots arrive, around May and June, small and delicate with their plume of green leaves. The second is most of the rest of the year. Maincrop carrots are harvested from August and, because they store well, are available through much of the winter. Unlike their relative the parsnip (*see p. 148*), carrots do not benefit from frost and are lifted and stored before the autumn frosts arrive. In February, when little in the garden is lovely, British carrots should be in good supply, whether they are lurking in your own root cellar or on sale from store at the local market.

Carrots have a relatively short history in this country, having been introduced in the fifteenth century in yellow or purple variants that were eventually succeeded by the contemporary orange carrot. Their recent history has been fraught. In the mid-1990s, carrots were found to contain high levels of pesticide residues and the government advised peeling and slicing off their tops in order to reduce the risk to consumers. The industry reacted, and residues are much less of an issue today. There are, however, stronger arguments for seeking out organically grown carrots: they are thought to taste better and contain less water. And it is good not to have to worry about peeling carrots, for their skin contains much of the flavour.

What to do with your comforting winter carrot is, of course, a matter of choice and taste. They are a useful ingredient in stock, and make a delightful mash when mixed with their seasonal fellows, swedes or turnips. Carrots contain a lot of sugar, so they also roast well, caramelizing sweetly like parsnips. This historically led to their being used as a substitute sweetener in hard times (also like parsnips). Today, it makes them a key ingredient of carrot cake, a rich and delightful thing that one can eat with a (largely unjustified) sense of virtue.

Growing your own carrots can be a tricky business. They like sandy soils and are particularly susceptible to the hard-to-kill carrot root fly that is the target of pesticides. Covering the plants with fleece or mesh keeps the pests off, and interplanting with onions or other smelly alliums can also deter them.

Chicory and endive

While they can be eaten all year round, chicory and its relative, endive, come in handy in the winter. Both are hardy and offer fresh, seasonal salady greenery at a time when fresh greenstuff is welcome. The bitterness of chicory in particular can be a little unsettling and is not to everyone's taste; however, it goes well with unexpected partners like rich soft cheese, and is mitigated by cooking.

There is such complexity surrounding the naming of chicory and endive that the *Oxford Companion to Food* includes an explanatory table. The types which turn up a lot in Britain are the curly endive, whose mad wig of leaves is available for much of the year; and radicchio, which has now become part of our gastronomic canon, having been a vegetable of vogue in the 1980s and 1990s. Also common are the headed 'sugarloaf' chicory, and the forced variety that goes by the splendid Belgian name of 'witloof'. This latter is treated like rhubarb and seakale (*see pp. 61 and 53*), its leaves cut off (in the autumn) then regrown, or replanted, and 'forced' in darkness to give a pale colour and less bitter flavour. Radicchio can be given a similar treatment, covered or grown in the dark so that its leaves, which in the light would tend to brownness, take on an attractive, rich red colour. Less common are the types of chicory grown for their roots, which, like those of its relative the dandelion, are used to make a substitute (or adulterant) for coffee.

Cooking chicory and endive seems the best way forward in a season when warmth and comfort are needed. For radicchio, a classic Italian treatment is to grill the trimmed and halved plants, top them with a cheese of your choice (and some prosciutto if needed) then grill briefly again, serving with the cheese bubbling and browned. For chicory, food writer Annie Bell suggests wilting the leaves in oil, or stuffing and braising the whole heads (or *chicons*). A classic witloof treatment is to bake a blanched *chicon* that has been wrapped in ham and covered in cheese sauce.

Onions

To include onions as a seasonal vegetable in February is definitely cheating. But here is a month that needs cheering up; and onions, despite their tear-jerking reputation, bring warmth and happiness with the depth, flavour and body they add to so many dishes. The fresh onion season in Britain runs from late summer until late autumn, but only gardeners are likely to eat onions straight from the ground. Doing so is quite a treat, for they are tender and excellent roasted or grilled on a barbecue.

The real strengths of onions are their ability to store for a long time; and then, of course, their enormous versatility in the kitchen. Once dug up, onions are traditionally dried in the sun until their skin achieves the familiar brown crispness. Then, to be stored, they are strung up or laid out in a cool, well-ventilated place where they will keep for months. The onions we eat are therefore mostly stored rather than fresh. Many of the onions we see in the shops will be from overseas; but there is no reason why we shouldn't still be feasting on stored British varieties in February and beyond. John Seymour, author of the *Complete Book of Self-sufficiency* and an apologist for most edible members of the allium family, says with customary lack of equivocation that 'Good food is inconceivable without onions.' Few in history have argued with this statement, although it has been suggested that a historic Indian taboo on onions for, among others, widows, students and Jains was related to the bulb's alleged aphrodisiac quality.

The use of onions in cooking merits a book in its own right. In February, however, it is to the comforting qualities of the onion that we should look. And while there are many good British recipes involving them, for once it is continental Europe that provides the best onion-based dishes for the cold months. The Alsatian dish of *tarte à l'oignon*, with its mixture of cream, meltingly soft onions and egg yolks, must be one of the richest vegetable dishes ever conceived; perfect for winter. And French onion soup (*see below*) makes a rich and warming meal in itself. Two onion tips: heating onions releases the sugars that provide so much flavour to dishes, but cooking them to sweet softness without burning can be difficult. A sprinkle of salt draws out enough juice to stop them catching. And don't discard the skins if you are making stock: they will add colour and flavour.

French onion soup

This classic, a warming, satisfying, tasty soup, is worth making in advance as it takes a bit of effort and improves if left for a day. This recipe gives an authentic result.

2kg/4lb onions, thinly sliced
100g/4oz butter
1/2 teaspoon sugar
2 litres/4 pints stock (beef is best, chicken will do)

heaped tablespoon flour
small glass dry white wine
salt and freshly ground pepper
3 tablespoons brandy

Melt 75g/3oz of the butter in a large heavy-bottomed pan, and sweat the sliced onions gently, covered, for 15 minutes, stirring occasionally. Turn up the heat, uncover the pan, sprinkle in the sugar and cook for 45 minutes, stirring regularly until the onions are golden brown, soft and dry.

Bring the stock to a simmer. In another small pan, melt the remaining 25g/1oz butter, stir in the flour, add two ladles of the hot stock and whisk until thick. Stir this into the remaining simmering stock.

Add the wine to the onions and cook until it has evaporated. Pour the stock over the onions and, stirring constantly, bring to a simmer. Season, and add the brandy. The soup is now ready to spend a day maturing.

Serve topped with croûtons made of French bread that has been cut into slices, laid out on a baking tray and baked for 15 minutes with a generous topping of grated cheese. Gruyère is traditional, but a mature cheddar might add a local note to this fine French soup.

Serves eight.

Rabbit

Fluffy, cute – and tasty. Rabbit doesn't have a formal closed season, but it's polite to leave them alone during their breeding season and when they're feeding young. So from September to around March at the latest, wild rabbits are an interesting addition to the seasonal larder. Farmed rabbits are available all year round; although the fact that they tend to be kept in cages like battery chickens and fed on pelleted food means that the farmed bunny makes a different meal to his wild counterpart: bigger, with a less gamey flavour and not as lean. It seems a shame, though, to eat rabbits that have been so kept, and thus encourage their confinement further. Surely it's better for both prey and cook if the rabbit has had an energetic alfresco life before ending up in a stew.

There used to be a massive surplus of rabbits (who are a serious agricultural pest, as Beatrix Potter's Mr McGregor knew only too well), brought on by the profusion of sheltering hedgerows that followed the acts of enclosure (*see p. 18*). In the early 1950s, however, the introduction of the myxomatosis virus wiped out 99 per cent of the population in two years. It has since recovered to around 37 million, and rabbits are back munching crops to the extent that farmers and landowners spend a good deal of time and effort controlling them, mainly through shooting and ferreting. Some of the output from this activity finds its way to game dealers and rural butchers, where those of us not inclined to take wild rabbit acquisition into our own hands are most likely to find them.

The process of 'paunching' (gutting) and skinning a rabbit in preparation for cooking is not to everyone's taste. Luckily, wild rabbits are always sold paunched, and often skinned and portioned. This of course means you miss out on the tasty offal as well as, possibly, the sartorial potential of the fur. It's no accident that a stew is the dish we perhaps associate the most with rabbit: the lean meat of the wild creatures can have a tendency to dryness, and older rabbits can be tough, so stewing makes the most of their flavour and texture.

Rhubarb, forced

Forced rhubarb puts some vibrant pink excitement into one of the British year's duller periods. Indeed, the original reason for the practice of rhubarb-forcing was to fill a gap in the dessert fruit calendar. But what is 'forcing'? In essence, it involves subjecting a plant to both heat and darkness so that tender shoots grow quickly in a desperate search for light. In the case of rhubarb, this has created one of the most bizarre forms of agriculture, in which large quantities of the plant are grown in long, low sheds, in almost total darkness; and harvested by hand, in candlelight. The rhubarb grows with such power that it makes a popping sound as the buds burst.

If all of this were not mysterious enough, the British industry is concentrated into a small area of West Yorkshire known as the 'Wakefield Triangle', whose other two corners are to the south and west of Leeds. A combination of heavy soils, readily available coal for heating, the right kind of weather, good transport links, and − yes − acid rain turned this otherwise agriculturally poor area into prime rhubarb-forcing territory. The area's cold autumns 'vernalize' the rhubarb roots ready for forcing so they can be lifted in mid-November and transplanted into sheds, where, in the warm darkness, pink sticks start to show after 4–6 weeks.

So important was the rhubarb industry in the mid-twentieth century that a 'rhubarb express' train used to carry hundreds of tonnes of the stuff down to eager consumers in the south. Today, the industry is much smaller, rhubarb's prominence having been diminished by imported exotic fruit, a dowdy, wartime image and the sheer expense of the labour-intensive forcing process. Still, it's readily available (if costly) and there is a resurgence of interest in this weird and wonderful plant, which is deemed infinitely better than its fresh counterpart (*see rhubarb, outdoor, p. 61*) by the fruit and veg cognoscenti. And if you want fresh British seasonal 'fruit' in February, it's about your only option.

Rhubarb fool

This is an easy way to create a delicately flavoured yet decadent dessert.

1kg/2lb forced rhubarb, chopped, leaves discarded
300g/11oz sugar
300ml/$^1/_2$ pint double cream

Preheat the oven to 180°C/350°F/gas 4. Place the rhubarb in an ovenproof dish, mix in the sugar and cook for 45 minutes until it is soft and much syrup has been liberated. Strain through a sieve, reserve the syrup, mash the rhubarb well with a fork and leave it to cool.

When it's cool (slightly warm will do, if you can't wait), stir in the cream, and serve. (Keep the syrup: it gives you another day's rhubarby dessert by making a perfect sauce for pouring over ice cream or mixing into yoghurt.) *Creates six modest yet rich portions.*

March

Treats for the month

March	Seasonal Treats	Coming in	Going out
Vegetables	Broccoli, purple sprouting Garlic, wild Nettles Onions, spring Seakale	Radishes Sorrel	Brussels sprouts Chicory Kale Leeks Parsnip
Fruit & Nuts			Rhubarb, forced
Meat, Game & Poultry			
Fish & Seafood	Elvers Scallops	Salmon, wild	Mussels

March

'As a sweet pledge of Spring the little lambs
Bleat in the varied weather round their dams'

It seems like it ought to be spring, but rarely feels like it. Even in these globally warming times, March remains the last breath of winter or, as Jane Grigson says the Irish once called it, the 'grey blast of spring'. Our ancestors were heading towards the 'hungry gap', when winter stores ran low and new produce had yet to mature.

Things are, however, looking up in March. Days are getting longer, with the equinox on 20–21 March marking the halfway point to the midsummer solstice. Even without real spring warmth, the longer days are encouraging more things to grow: elder and hawthorn trees are coming into leaf, daffodils appear, and those of us with lawns may need to fire up the mower. In response to these signals of spring, birds get noisier as they nest, and bees go in search of early flowers and blossoms. Lambing continues, occurring later the further north (and the higher up) the creatures are raised. Calving, which can happen all year round, is concentrated in the spring. It's also muckspreading time on the farm, and a month when crops are fertilized and sprayed. Things are getting a little thin in the seasonal food store, with some winter brassicas giving up the ghost. There are many good things, though: wild garlic and sorrel for the adventurous, scallops and wild salmon for the moneyed and purple sprouting broccoli for everyone.

Broccoli, purple sprouting

It seems unlikely that a humble broccoli, a vegetable so often associated with sulphurous mass-catering mush, could provoke much excitement. But the arrival of the purple sprouting variety in early spring should rightly be a cause for celebration among seasonally fixated eaters: one does, eventually, tire of roots and cabbage, even of leeks, so the novelty of this handsome brassica is always welcome. Purple sprouting broccoli is a tough and hardy plant, hence its ability to withstand the winter and be ready to delight us in February and March. This also means we have multiple opportunities through the year for in-season broccoli, for its relatives calabrese (the more familiar green, large-headed broccoli, *see p. 102*) and the fractal-patterned bright green romanesco are ready in the summer and autumn.

So esteemed is purple sprouting broccoli as a gourmet vegetable that it is often compared to asparagus, with which it shares a delicacy of flavour and texture as well as a brevity of season. Unlike asparagus, it is relatively easy to grow, and it's hard to beat the freshness of your own crop: picked straight off the plant, the heads are even good to eat raw. It's customary to cook them, though, but only lightly: purple sprouting broccoli is rich in goodness and, like any broccoli, will quickly achieve the feared canteen sogginess if overcooked. Brief steaming, then, or blanching is the way to deal with it, whereafter it should be eaten immediately, maybe with pepper and butter, should you feel the need to add anything at all.

Elvers

A seasonal meal whose decline in numbers and commercial exploitation mean few today will get to eat them, elvers (or glass eels) were once a major delicacy. Elvers are the young eels (*see p. 125*), which enter European rivers after a three-year drift across the Atlantic ocean from the Sargasso Sea in which they were born. Sensitive to fresh water and to temperature, elvers enter south-western rivers, in particular the Severn and the Wye, in March and April. The lucky ones spend years maturing in Britain's rivers before their internal clock tells them to return to the sea to spawn. Less fortunate elvers – the only fish 'fry' (young) that can legally be taken as food in Britain – are caught by hand nets from jealously guarded, licensed riverside fishing spots called 'tumps'.

Elvers are a serious business: at their peak in 1997–8 exports were worth £2.6m, and together with eels they make up the country's most valuable inland fishery. Not that the bulk of Britain's elver catch is eaten, though: it supplies eel farming in Europe and Asia. So a March breakfast of elvers fried in bacon fat is a realistic prospect only for residents of the South-west who are friendly with an elver-fishing licence holder; or for enthusiasts prepared to buy in bulk. With prices up to £200 per kilo recorded, you really have to want your elvers badly. While elver catches have remained reasonably constant over recent years, there is strong evidence that populations are crashing, down to as little as 1 per cent of former levels. Over-exploitation is only part of the story: the impact of climate change on the strength of the Gulf Stream may also be affecting elver arrivals in Europe. The future for elvers is uncertain, but it seems likely that their status as a seasonal food will become a historical footnote.

Garlic, wild

Stinking Nanny, we used to call it in my Derbyshire childhood: wild garlic (or ramsons) has a host of other vaguely pejorative names in different counties. It never occurred to us then that this pungent plant of damp woodland was something that could be eaten. It's a lot to do with the smell. Wild garlic tends to cover quite large areas and in such concentrations that its garlicky aroma is strong enough to perfume the entire woodland, leading one to assume that to eat it would be a dangerously overpowering experience. Its flavour is in fact milder than the smell would lead one to expect; akin to the commercially grown garlic to which it is related.

Common throughout Britain, wild garlic starts to appear in March or earlier, and its attractive white flowers grow from April to June. So along with nettles (*see below*), it is one of the British season's first fresh green treats. The youngest leaves can be eaten raw in salads, added as flavouring to soups and stews, or used to wrap lamb before roasting. The leaves are also used to wrap (and thus flavour) cheeses, notably a wild garlic variant of the more commonly nettle-wrapped Cornish Yarg. Dedicated wild garlic fans can even seek out the bulbs later in the summer, although the attractions of 'wet' garlic (*see p. 79*) might be too much of a distraction.

Nettles

Eat nettles? Why? Because they're good for you, that's why. And because in bleak March, there's not much else that's new and fresh on offer for the seasonal gourmet. Nettles are around for much of the growing season but young ones make the best eating and after June chemical changes make them coarse, bitter and – as *Food for Free* author Richard Mabey warns – 'decidedly laxative'. Best eat them early, then. The formic acid that gives nettles their sting is destroyed by cooking, so nettle dishes need not be the subject of macho eating competitions. Nettles do, however, contain histamines and other beneficial substances that are known for their purifying qualities, as well as lowering blood pressure and having a toning effect on the body.

Together with the lack of other fresh seasonal greenery, all of this goodness is a fine reason to grasp the nettle in March. Do wear gloves though: heavy-duty rubber ones give the best combination of protection and manual dexterity and remain necessary right up until the nettles are cooked. Finding nettles is very rarely a problem, as they grow throughout Britain and have a particular affinity with urban waste ground. You should seek out short young shoots, or the palest young leaves. Now you have a groaning carrier bag of nettles sitting on the kitchen table, what to do with it?

Things to do with nettles: They can be cooked like spinach – the leaves should be separated from their stalks and, of course, washed well before being wilted down in a little water and served with butter. A compressed fistful of cooked nettles can be chopped finely and added to a fresh pasta mix to create the livid green pasta of your choice. The washed leaves can be tossed into a panful of stock and stock vegetables, cooked, then blended to make a good soup. You can even turn nettles into beer, which seems a good payback for a lifetime of being stung. Nettles also feature in Dock Pudding, a mixture of early wild greens, herbs and oatmeal whose charms are the subject of much equivocation and also a lively competition in Yorkshire's Calder Valley (*see p. 24*).

Onions, spring

Spring onions, confusingly, have a long season, but their arrival in early spring brings a sharp new freshness to an otherwise bleak time of year. Also called scallions, they are mostly immature onions (*see p. 41*) harvested around eight weeks after planting and eaten fresh rather than dried. Like so many vegetables today, spring onions are available all year round, thanks to imports and high-tech growing techniques, but fresh, outdoor British spring onions make a welcome seasonal treat. Their outdoor season extends well beyond spring because they can be sown 'successionally', providing a constant crop until the autumn frosts kick in.

A popular way with spring onions is to use them raw, where their flavour can add interest to salads; however, unless used sparingly they can be overpowering to the eater (and to the eater's friends). Like fresh full-grown onions or 'wet' garlic (*see p. 79*), spring onions can impart a more subtle flavour to dishes when cooked. Spring onions – or their close relatives – are a mainstay of Asian cuisine, where they are almost always cooked. Perhaps we should cook them a little more over here. *The River Café Cook Book Green* suggests braising them in chicken stock with the first of the season's peas; or using them with thin-sliced new potatoes as a pizza topping. Not very British-sounding, admittedly; but delicious and very seasonal.

Scallops

When should one eat a scallop? The views of conservationists, seafood experts and fishmongers seem to diverge. Scallops are available all year round, but a couple of factors suggest the best time to eat them. They spawn from April to September; and like all bivalve molluscs (*see also mussels, p. 137, and oysters, p. 126*) they are susceptible to toxic algal blooms which tend to appear during the warmer months. However, the waters in which they are commercially cultivated are strictly monitored and scallops are highly unlikely ever to present any danger to the buyer. Autumn and winter still seems to be the best time to seek out scallops, though, especially because in the very late winter one needs the cheer that such an exquisite delicacy can bring.

Some bizarre scallop facts: 'King' and the smaller 'Queen' scallops are not male and female, but different species, for the scallop is a hermaphrodite. You can tell the age of a King (or Great) scallop – whose shell has one flat and one curved side – by counting the rings on the flat side. Once mature, scallops are 'free-swimming', using the mighty muscle that is their main gastronomic attraction to open and shut their shell and propel themselves through the water.

Buying scallops, as with most seafood, is a difficult business if one is concerned both about the quality of the product and the sustainability of the harvest. Dredging – which accounts for most of the scallops commercially sold – is hugely destructive to the seabed, and can damage the scallop and fill its shell with gritty debris. Diver-caught scallops, maybe 10 per cent of the catch, tend to be of a higher quality and the process is benign to the environment.

> *Cooking scallops:* For the perfect scallop experience, scallops should be bought in their shells to guarantee freshness. Opening the shells and removing the unwanted bits requires a bit of effort but, like shucking oysters, it is effort well rewarded. As a bonus, you get to keep the most decorative, 'shell-like' shells available. Cooking scallops is all about speed and simplicity. They have an affinity with bacon, sage and – strangely – Jerusalem artichokes (*see p. 146*) whose season they largely share. A minute or so of hot frying on either side creates a sweetly caramelized delicacy that should be eaten straight away.

Seakale

Together with watercress, samphire and possibly parsnip, seakale is one of only a few vegetables that are truly native to the British Isles. Everything else, as Jane Grigson points out in *English Food*, has been imported over the centuries and developed to suit our climate. It's a good job we don't depend on seakale for our sustenance today, because it is very difficult to obtain. Nothing at all to do with kale (*see p. 30*), seakale grows wild on sand and shingle beaches, and its stalks and leaves were originally eaten like cabbage. The interesting bits of seakale, however, are the tender, blanched stalks that develop beneath the sand or shingle. These have a delicate, nutty flavour that has been compared to asparagus but they are sweeter and more juicy in texture. They are cooked and eaten in a similar way to asparagus (*see p. 68*).

The problem with seakale is scarcity. In the nineteenth century the plants were covered over with shingle or sand so that the tender stalks were 'forced', and these were then sent on to commercial markets. Seakale's popularity took off to such an extent that the wild supply was radically depleted, and it is now illegal to harvest it in the wild. Commercially grown seakale is available on a small-scale basis, and it can also be grown and forced by keen gardeners. The process is similar to that used for forced rhubarb (*see p. 43*): the seakale crowns are exposed to frost then forced under cover in a darkened shed. Traditionally, seakale was forced under terracotta pots. Both old and new methods are time-consuming and expensive; they contribute to seakale's status as a very rare seasonal delicacy.

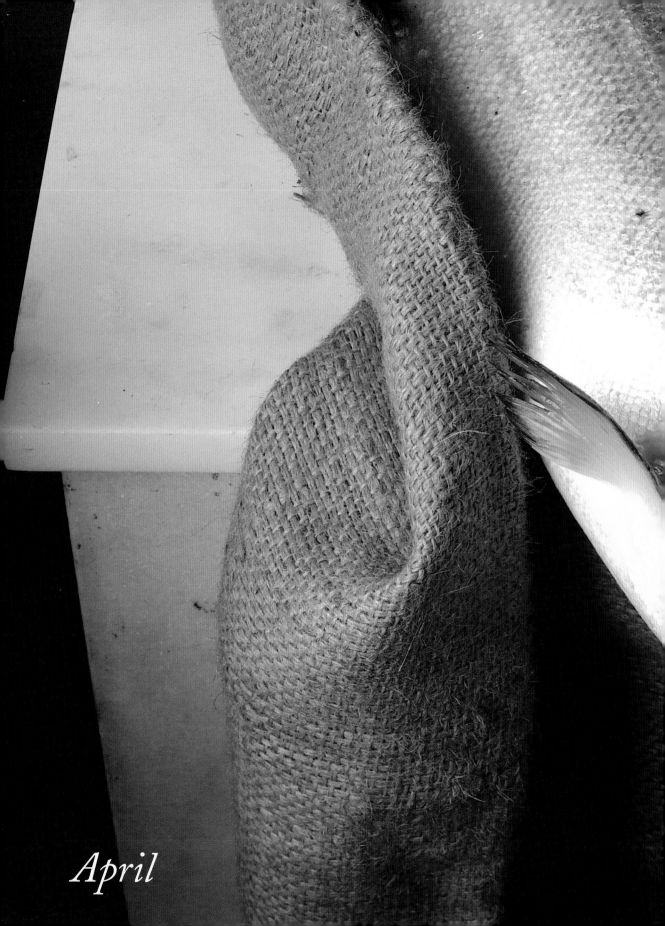

April

Treats for the month

April	Seasonal Treats	Coming in	Going out
Vegetables	Dandelion Mushrooms, morel Potatoes Spring greens	Watercress	Broccoli, purple sprouting Garlic, wild
Fruit & Nuts	Rhubarb, outdoor		
Meat, Game & Poultry	Wood pigeon		
Fish & Seafood	Salmon, wild	Crab, brown Sea trout	Oysters, native

April

*'The blossoms open one by one
And sunny hours beguile'*

Spring finally gets into its stride in April. The weather may be unsettled, but it's warming noticeably; and the countryside responds by taking on a mantle of vivid green as trees and hedgerows come into leaf. More blossom arrives, with blackthorn (sloe) and damson trees a spectacular sight. And another colourful feature of the contemporary British landscape appears: winter-sown oilseed rape starts to turn much of the countryside yellow. Farmers will be fertilizing fields to encourage grass growth for hay and silage, and planting winter fodder crops.

Despite all its verdure and promise, mid-April marked the beginning of the year's leanest time for our forebears: the 'hungry gap' that extended through until the next staple crops were ready in June. At this time of year, winter stores were much depleted and there was little fresh produce. Today, the only people likely to be bothered by the hungry gap are hardcore smallholders or subscribers to vegetable box schemes, the more purist of which don't operate from April to June.

April's seasonal specialities are eclectic. Jersey Royals are the first new potatoes to appear, courtesy of their latitude and the seaweed that fertilizes them. Morel mushrooms buck the autumn wild mushroom trend by appearing in the spring to those lucky or skilled enough to find them. Dandelions offer a fresh, free salad treat. Outdoor rhubarb comes in as the first 'natural' fruit of the British season, even though it's a vegetable. And the now rare spring treats of elvers and sea trout lurk in our rivers.

Dandelion

Here's one wild delicacy you won't have any trouble finding. There's no particular reason to include dandelions in April, beyond the fact that this is when the bright yellow flowers are typically in profusion, as a reminder that here lurks something good to eat. It's not the flowers, though; these are traditionally used to make beer or wine. Young dandelion leaves, which make a flavoursome addition to salads, are the main attraction. Dandelion leaves grow throughout the year, providing a constant tasty wild harvest as long as only the youngest leaves, towards the plant's centre, are used: the older, outer leaves tend to be bitter.

Dandelion is renowned for health-giving properties, particularly as a blood purifier; but its French name, *pissenlit*, alludes to its less welcome diuretic quality. Dandelion should not be eaten in great quantity. Those wishing to get the most out of their wild harvest can also dry, roast and grind dandelion roots, which are said to make a passable, caffeine-free imitation of coffee; the roots can also be eaten as a vegetable. And gardeners irritated by dandelions infesting pristine lawns can inflict gourmet revenge on them by covering the plants and forcing them, rhubarb-style, in order to create more tender and tasty leaves. The French *salade de pissenlit* sits fried bacon chunks atop raw dandelion leaves and should probably not be eaten too close to bedtime.

Mushrooms, morel

Don't go asking a wild mushroom dealer for morels in the autumn: if you're lucky, you will be politely reminded that, unlike the vast majority of British wild fungi, morels are a springtime delicacy, appearing from March to May. As well as being out of seasonal synch with most of our other wild mushrooms, morels also look very different to most people's idea of a mushroom, for their cap is thin and wrinkly and has been likened to a 'coarse sponge', and their stems are short. Morels favour sandy and chalky soil and are said to be fond of burnt ground, so much so that in eighteenth-century Germany forest fires resulted from peasants' attempts to create advantageous morel-growing conditions. They have, however, resisted attempts at cultivation and their relative scarcity can mean a monster price tag for those going morel-shopping. The fine, gourmet flavour of morels no doubt has an influence on their price too, for they are a seasonal treat well worth seeking out. Should you be lucky enough to find them in the wild, you don't have to eat them all at once, because morels can be threaded on strings and dried, whereafter they keep well. That said, a big morel feast is a fine idea: you can buy dried ones any time. Recipes for morels abound, many of them complex and creamy. In *Wild Food*, Roger Phillips suggests serving them on fried bread, an unpretentious, delicious and very British dish.

Morels on fried bread

A modest but luxurious first course. Beware the quantity of morels, which will be terrifically expensive. Bulking out the dish with less aristocratic mushrooms is fine.

250g/8oz mushrooms
50g/2oz butter
a little stock
chopped parsley and thyme

salt and freshly ground pepper
1 egg yolk
3 tablespoons double cream
bread

Wash and clean the mushroom caps in running water, remove the stem-bases, dry thoroughly and split lengthways. If using dried morels, reconstitute in warm water for 20 minutes, reserving the water for stock.

Stew for 30 minutes in the butter and stock, a little chopped parsley and thyme, salt and pepper. Stir in the egg yolk and cream to thicken.
Serve on bread fried in bacon fat.
Serves four.

Potatoes

What have potatoes done to deserve a mention in a book about seasonal food? After all, they are a constant, year-round staple and Britons eat more of them per head than any other European country, Ireland included. While you could happily eat potatoes all year without a care for the season, a little knowledge about their seasonality and their varieties can radically improve your potato experience.

In spite of their central status in the British diet, potatoes have been with us for only a relatively short time, arriving from South America in the sixteenth century and regarded with deep distrust (like tomatoes, they are related to deadly nightshade) for a long time thereafter. They were gradually accepted and became, like parsnips before them, a standby winter crop in case of poor grain harvests; however, potatoes were not truly established as a popular British food until the nineteenth century. Their food value and ease of growing and cooking led to potatoes' becoming such a staple in nineteenth-century Ireland that much of the rural population ate little else, consuming up to 5 kilos (14lb) of potatoes per head each day. The terrible famine triggered when the crops were devastated by potato blight (a highly destructive disease that continues to menace crops today) is an extreme example of the danger of relying on a single crop. Nowadays, we're not reliant on potatoes but they are perhaps more significant to the British diet than anything else.

So how are potatoes seasonal? There are two main types, distinguished by how long they take to mature and how quickly they are eaten after harvest. 'Earlies', more commonly known as 'new' potatoes, mature the quickest and are harvested from June onwards (or as early as April for Jersey Royals, which are helped by the island's warm climate). Earlies are a seasonal treat because they are tender, sweetly tasty and a natural accompaniment to other early-summer seasonal foods. They are often defined as 'waxy', making them ideal for boiling and using in salads. Waxy potatoes are also perfect for *gratin dauphinois*, a dish which gloriously obsessive food writer Jeffrey Steingarten goes to phenomenal lengths to perfect in his book *It Must Have Been Something I Ate*. Longer-maturing 'maincrop' potatoes, harvested in the autumn and then stored for months, provide the larger varieties which we use for almost every other purpose. They tend to be 'floury', better for mashing, baking, roasting and chipping. Their skins 'set', so need to be peeled rather than scrubbed, although peeling risks removing much of the goodness and flavour which lurks just millimetres beneath the skin. Any green skin on potatoes should be removed, though, or the spud should not be eaten at all: it means the potato has been left out too long in the light and contains solanin, which is poisonous.

Few British people need advice on how to cook potatoes; everyone has a favourite method. The use of goose fat (*see p. 111*) is strongly recommended as a major step on the way to roast potato heaven, though. The table opposite gives an overview of popular varieties, their uses and their seasons.

Gratin Dauphinois

This is adapted from Jeffrey Steingarten's microscopically detailed recipe.

250ml/1/2 pint milk
1 garlic clove, peeled and crushed
salt and freshly ground pepper
12 gratings of fresh nutmeg
a small knob of butter

700g/1lb 8oz waxy potatoes
(see chart), peeled and sliced
into 3mm rounds
300ml/1/2 pint double cream

Preheat the oven to 220°C/425°F/gas 7.

Boil the milk with the crushed garlic, some ground black pepper, a large pinch of salt and the grated nutmeg. Remove from the heat.

Liberally butter a large, low baking dish (Steingarten recommends a cast-iron version with an area of 300 square cm/120 square inches but – and I know such licence is not the point in his recipes – use what you can). Arrange the sliced potatoes in a single layer, in rows overlapping like roof tiles. If you have some left over, do something else with them. Bring the milk to the boil again and strain it over the potatoes, removing the garlic.

Bake the potatoes in the oven for 15 minutes, or until most of the milk is absorbed. Then bring the double cream to the boil and pour that over the potatoes. Bake for a further 20–25 minutes until the potatoes are golden brown dotted with thickened cream. Let it settle for 10 minutes, and then eat immediately, for, as Steingarten warns, 'taste and texture suffer with each passing minute'.

Serves six as a side dish.

Potato varieties and their seasons

	First early (April–July)	Second early (July–Aug)	Maincrop (Sept–Oct and stored through winter)
Waxy: Boiling Salads Gratins Frying	Arran Pilot Jersey Royal Maris Bard Pentland Javelin	Charlotte Estima Maris Piper	Pink Fir Apple
Floury: Baking Mashing		Wilja	Cara, Golden Wonder King Edward Maris Piper, Romano Pentland Squire
Dry, firm: Chips Roasting			Desiree (red-skinned) Golden Wonder King Edward Pentland Crown
All-rounders		Charlotte	Desiree King Edward Maris Piper Pentland Dell

Rhubarb, outdoor

British outdoor rhubarb appears in April, just when the supplies of delicate, pink forced rhubarb (*see p. 43*), which have been going since January, start to dry up. Aficionados of the fancy pink stuff may turn up their noses at the tougher outdoor rhubarb, but it is not without its merits. For a start, there's nothing else in the way of fresh seasonal fruit available in this still-sparse time, so it makes for a useful treat. (Rhubarb is botanically classed as a vegetable, but is considered a fruit for its main usage as a dessert.) Fresh rhubarb is more astringent than forced; this somehow seems to suit the season and makes it interesting in a different way. It can partner oily fish as gooseberries do, as well as making a good pudding.

Rhubarb is around early because it is suited to Britain's temperate climate. It is particularly light-sensitive, and grows in response to lengthening days rather than being reliant on heat for its 'ripening'. Its crowns (or rhizomes), from which the edible stems grow, are not bothered by frost and the plant is a perennial, so, once planted, rhubarb can go on producing indefinitely. And one plant is all you need to provide all the rhubarb a family wants, should you wish to grow it at home. It can take up a lot of space, but is easy to grow and will thrive happily atop a pile of manure if necessary. You can force rhubarb yourself, covering the crown with a tall pot in January so that more tender shoots appear in a desperate search for light. It seems a shame, though, thus to deprive the Yorkshire rhubarb-forcing industry of custom, particularly when their product will almost inevitably be superior. Rhubarb leaves contain a toxic concentration of oxalic acid and should be composted rather than eaten.

There are many different ways with rhubarb, but the obvious ones are the best: stewing with a little water and sugar until soft and then serving with custard; or making it into a rhubarb crumble, a pudding which manages to be both comforting and refreshing, ideal for the uncertain weather of April.

Salmon, wild

It may not look it, but salmon is a terrifically political creature. Whether or not to eat it – and what sort of salmon to eat – are questions that plague any ethically minded gourmet today. Farmed salmon is, of course, available all year round, and relatively cheap. It can be good, but rarely approaches the quality of the wild fish. Quite apart from concerns over what toxins it may have ingested in its feed, there's the question of the impact of farmed salmon, from its effects on wild stocks and local ecosystems, to the use of chemicals and drugs in its production. And with 3kg of wild fish generally needed to produce 1kg of farmed salmon, there has surely to be a serious question about the long-term sustainability of aquaculture.*

The seeker after a true seasonal salmon treat should go looking for the wild variant of *Salmo salar*, the Atlantic salmon. Here, though, a dilemma remains: stocks have declined by 67 per cent in the past thirty years as the noble fish has been under siege from pollution, soil runoff, fish farming and now climate change. But we should pursue wild salmon on the basis that demand encourages supply, because supply – in this case – means ensuring the very survival of an endangered wild species. And what a fascinating, beautiful specimen the Atlantic salmon is. Its lifestyle is an epic tale of struggle. It spawns in the gravel beds of freshwater rivers, where the young spend up to three years before migrating to the sea. After covering huge distances to feed, adult salmon return to the rivers in which they were born in order to spawn. The smaller salmon returning for the first time are known as grilse. Although many die after spawning, those that return for a second or third time are the ones prized by game anglers and serious gourmets.

While seasons vary in rivers around the country, wild salmon tends to be available from the end of February to the end of August. It's expensive, but it has earned its price. How to eat it? With reverence. Smoked wild salmon is widely available; and a whole fresh fish would make a superb centrepiece to a spring banquet.

*It would be unfair to discuss salmon aquaculture without reference to organic production, for which standards have now been established. The fish are still farmed, for sure, but with better husbandry – lower stocking densities, more 'natural' feeding cycles – and no pesticides or drugs. Perhaps most importantly, the feed must be from sustainable sources: currently this is from the by-products (i.e. the trimmings and offal) of wild fish caught for human consumption.

Spring greens

Eat your greens! Spring greens are one of the first green things to arrive in the natural British vegetable season. Because of this, and the fact that they are fresh-tasting and highly nutritious, one should be able to welcome and eat them without the need for the traditional parental coercion. Along with red and savoy cabbage (*see pp. 147 and 40 and the cabbage seasonality table below*), spring greens are one of the cabbage varieties that qualify for seasonal treat status. As with other members of the brassica family such as kale, broccoli and Brussels sprouts, cabbage really is good for you, being rich in potassium, iron and vitamins A, C and E. So go on, eat your greens. With something of spinach about them, spring greens are light and fresh in comparison to heavier winter cabbage and are a fine companion to early-spring lunches and dinners. Simple, short steaming is all they need to provide a tasty and healthy bit of spring greenery.

The seasonality of cabbages

VARIETY	J	F	M	A	M	J	J	A	S	O	N	D
Spring				○	○							
Summer						○	○	○				
Autumn									○	○	○	○
Winter White	●	●	●								○	○
Savoy	○	○	○							○	○	○
Savoy hybrids	○	○	○							○	○	○
January King	○	○									○	○
Red	●	●								○	○	○

○ Picked Fresh   ● From Store

Source: *Vegetables*, Phillips and Rix

Wood pigeon

Wood pigeon is not strictly a seasonal treat, as it is legal for the bird to be shot all year round. This is because, despite their grace and beauty, wood pigeon are a major agricultural pest and lumped together with the brown rat, crow, magpie and others in a rogues' gallery of creatures for whom the open season is any season. However, come the spring, there's food in sufficient abundance to turn a scrawny wood pigeon into a plump and tasty meal. As with squirrels, one should feel no qualms about taking up arms (with the proper permission) against wood pigeon, for the UK population is estimated at about twenty million. Happily, they are also widely available through good butchers and game dealers. And one advantage they have over almost all of the classier game birds is that they are likely to be truly wild, and therefore largely additive-free.

Young birds make a tasty roast and need to be larded well to stop them drying out. Or their breasts can be fast-fried to make a gamey pink steak. Their carcasses produce rich stock and older birds can be casseroled or turned into an elaborate pie.

May

Treats for the month

May	Seasonal Treats	Coming in	Going out
Vegetables	Asparagus Radishes Rocket Sorrel	Beans, broad Beetroot Peas	Mushrooms, morel Nettles Seakale
Fruit & Nuts		Elderflower	
Meat, Game & Poultry	Rook	Lamb, new season	
Fish & Seafood	Crab, brown		

May

'Come queen of months in company
Wi' all thy merry minstrelsy'

May is the peak of spring, a time of wild fertility when the countryside is bright green with new leaves, scented with blossom and loud in the early mornings with a noisy dawn chorus of nesting birds. The beginning of the month was celebrated by the Celts (and is still marked by Scots and contemporary pagans) as Beltane, a fire festival to honour this blooming fertility of the land and the promise of summer fruitfulness to come. The May Day festivities that are better known in England also celebrate fertility, with maypole dancing, and 'beating the bounds' ceremonies to ask for a blessing on the crops.

This is the best month for blossom of all kinds, with horse chestnut trees and many fruit trees in flower, and abundant hawthorn blossom that can even cheer up motorways. Our food chain is busy, with rapid crop growth on the farms and the fields now full of grazing, fattening livestock. May is also the time when the seasonal food year starts to get serious. The arrival this month of English asparagus should be carved into every gourmet's diary, for it is a delightful but fleeting pleasure, best enjoyed as near to the source as possible. There are also the first crops of peas and beans to enjoy; and peppery radishes and rocket are ready, together with fresh, young beetroot. Agile, committed carnivores could go climbing a rookery for an unusual seasonal treat; and as summer approaches, it's a good time to be thinking about a crustacean feast too.

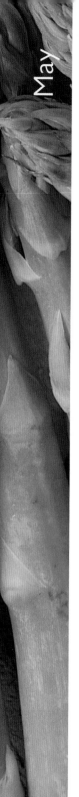

Asparagus

Blink and you'll miss it. Our asparagus is so good, yet so ephemeral, that not to have its season burnt into my brain seemed a terrible omission. So here it is: the British asparagus season formally starts on 1 May and lasts for little more than six weeks. Depending on the weather, it can start later, or as early as mid-April. The season traditionally ends on midsummer's day. But May and early June are the times to find British asparagus.

Why is it such a big deal? First, there's its gourmet quality. It is rightly deemed the most delicious of all vegetables for its delicate, subtle taste and tender texture. Asparagus has been esteemed by gourmets since Roman times and by the seventeenth century London was surrounded by asparagus growers who fed the city's appetite for the delicacy. The centre of asparagus gravity eventually moved to the market gardening area of the Vale of Evesham, and today Evesham remains identified with asparagus, even though much commercial cultivation now happens in the east of England. The green asparagus we in Britain like grows more slowly, so the spears develop a fuller flavour and better texture; a much superior product, many claim, to the larger blanched asparagus favoured by the French and Germans.

A further, crucial reason for the importance of the season is that asparagus does not keep or store. Once cut, its quality deteriorates rapidly because like peas (*see p. 83*) its tasty sugars soon begin converting to starch. Unlike peas, however, it doesn't freeze well. So if you want asparagus at its very, very best, you need to eat it as soon after picking as possible. Which means that either growing your own or touring the growing areas for roadside stalls in May are the best options; seeking out good greengrocers and farmers' markets is second best; and buying supermarket asparagus, even in season, comes third. The 'hub and spoke', packaged, palletized distribution system used by supermarkets almost inevitably means that their asparagus will have spent too much time on the road. And as for buying imported asparagus out of season, there's just one word: why?

Asparagus is also a big deal because it's hard to grow. It takes a few years for a bed to become fully productive, and even then the yield is relatively low. Asparagus needs its own dedicated space and does not fit into any crop rotations; and it has to be hand-harvested with special knives. It also shares with beetroot (*see p. 78*) a disturbing effect on the eater's urine. In the case of asparagus, it can endow it with an unusual smell. This potentially off-putting factor (to prudish British eaters), together with asparagus's gourmet qualities and the effort of growing it, created a mystique, expense and aristocratic reputation that for a while put the British public off their finest vegetable. As Jane Grigson lamented of asparagus in her 1971 book *Good Things*: 'Are we of all the people in Europe so cowed by past grandeur that we cling to cabbages and to giant, stringy scarlet runners and olympian marrows?' Happily, the paltry 1,000 acres of British asparagus-growing she cited then had doubled by 2001: it seems her passionate advocacy has worked.

Cooking asparagus: This remains surrounded by an unnecessary degree of fiddle and faff that often accompanies great gourmet foods. In reality, you do not need a special kettle to cook it. The key is to get it as fresh as possible, break off the woody ends of the spears (great for stock), peel the spears only if they are really thick; then just throw them in a big pan of boiling water for 3–5 minutes before serving with a dip of melted butter, bacon fat or vinaigrette. Asparagus also makes superb risotto (*see p. 32*) if the chopped stalks are added early for flavour and the blanched tips added just at the end.

Crab, brown

The brown (or edible) crab is the big, pie-shelled crustacean that we most commonly eat. Is there a particularly good time to crack into one? They are not sharply seasonal, but as crabs spawn in the winter, this, together with the fact that crab-eating seems so much a warm-weather pastime, makes spring and summer seem the best time to eat them.

Catching an edible crab yourself is not easy. They tend to live in deeper, offshore waters and are caught commercially in very deep-laid pots (or creels). If anything, British brown crabs are more regional than seasonal. Those from the south coast of Devon can weigh up to 3kg and are second in size only to Alaskan king crabs, the world's biggest. Crabs from Cromer in Norfolk are rated by gourmets and noted for their sweetness, while crabs from the east coast of Scotland are thought best of all for their rich feeding in cold, (relatively) unpolluted water. So it is worth finding out about your crab's provenance, as well as consulting the calendar, when going crab-shopping.

Unlike lobster (*see p. 94*), crab tends to be sold cooked (boiled) and as there is a risk this may have been overdone, it is worth finding live crabs. The vexed question of slaughter is thus raised: as with lobster, a plunge into boiling water will do the job but may also affect the quality of the crab's meat as well as resulting in the claws being shed. A spike between the eyes and another under the 'apron' – the small flap beneath the carapace – will finish it off, whereafter it can be boiled, like lobster. Male (cock) crabs, identifiable by a narrower and more pointed apron, are better eating. It is also best to find a crab with a bit of wear and tear (worn claws, the odd barnacle). Crabs cannot grow their shells, so they shed them periodically, leaving behind a hollow discarded exoskeleton. A crab that hasn't moulted for a while – and is thus looking a bit weathered – will be meatier than one with a brand new shell.

There are many recipes for crab, the most startling of which is an old British custom, cited by Jane Grigson, of 'tunnel boning' a leg of lamb and stuffing the cavity with crab meat before roasting. Given that anchovy is a famous improver of lamb, this should not be a surprising suggestion; but it's one for the committed, nonetheless. Far simpler to treat a crab feast as an adventure in messy, tooled-up deconstruction accompanied by fine, chilled white wine. The sweet brown meat of the shell and firmer white meat of the legs and claws make two separate delicacies.

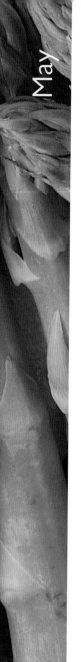

Crab is widely available, but, as with many marine species, under severe pressure. The current fishery accounts for 60 per cent of the stock annually, an unsustainable level that is being addressed by a licensing scheme introduced in 2004. Hopefully this will ensure that the fine summer feast of brown crab stays on our plates.

A footnote: if a search for brown crab turns up a spider crab instead, then you are lucky indeed. Hugely esteemed by the French and Spanish, who know a thing or two about seafood (and take much of our catch), spider crabs prefer warmer waters but sometimes turn up in south-west England. Despite their scary, leggy appearance, they are delicious.

Dressed crab

For those seeking to present the crab and its contents in a way that removes the effort for the dinner guest, 'dressing' it is the solution. It's also a way of being sure that your dressed crab contains no unwanted seasoning or extras: the bought stuff may well have been diluted with a few too many breadcrumbs. There are all sorts of fancy ways of dressing a crab, involving multiple ingredients and artful presentation; however, given the effort of extracting the meat, simplest is best.

1 (cooked) crab per person
lemon juice
fine, fresh breadcrumbs

salt and pepper
mayonnaise (optional)

Turn the crab on its back and separate the body (to which the legs are attached) from the shell. Remove the mouth part and the attached stomach bag and the grey, feathery 'dead men's fingers', and discard these.

Now for the edible stuff. Scoop out the rich brown meat from within the shell and put it to one side; then, using whatever tools take your fancy, remove the white meat from the claws, legs and body. Mix the brown meat with a tablespoonful of breadcrumbs, a squeeze of lemon juice and some salt and pepper; the white meat can be left plain or seasoned and mixed with a dollop of mayonnaise.

The shell, suitably cleaned and tidied, forms a perfect bowl for the crab meat. Good brown bread and butter completes the dish; a fine, dry, chilled white wine turns it into a perfect moment.

Radishes

Radishes are not big in Britain. In oriental countries large radishes such as daikon or mooli are popular, and these can be found in specialist greengrocers here. However, the radish to which we have traditionally taken is the small, peppery salad radish, eaten raw. Radishes are related to turnips and to horseradish, and contain a substance similar to that found in mustard, hence the often fiery taste. Fresh radish leaves also have a wonderful peppery flavour and are a great clue to the freshness of your bunch.

Another seasonal treat for the amateur gardener, radishes are famous for being very easy and quick to grow. Some varieties can mature in a month or less and a successional sowing will give you a constant supply through the summer. Radishes can be chopped up and added to salads, or dipped in relishes; but the practice of halving them and dipping them in salt, which rounds out their hot, nutty flavour, takes some beating.

Rocket

Peppery, and with a marvellous name, rocket is a seasonal treat worth waiting for. Of course, like many salad vegetables, it is available all year round in supermarkets. And there are varieties that can be sown in the autumn to survive a mild winter. It's worth waiting for, though, because nothing you buy in the shops is likely to beat the taste, satisfaction and economy of your own crop.

The best time to sow rocket is in March and April, so, with six weeks before the plant is fully grown, May is likely to be the time when rocket starts to feature in your life. Apart from its excellent, often strong flavour, the main reason for growing rocket is that it is extremely easy and rewarding to do so. It takes up little effort or space and requires minimal horticultural skill. The plant grows fast and when cut, more leaves grow back, giving you a constant harvest until it bolts (goes to seed) in the summer heat and the leaves become stalky and bitter.

Rocket has a short history as a British seasonal delicacy, having become hysterically fashionable in restaurants in the 1980s and 1990s. Our attitude to rocket has now settled down and it has earned its place as one of the most interesting of salad ingredients. Rocket has a peppery 'bite' that gets stronger as its leaves get bigger. While a salad of pure rocket can be a little intense for some, it is nonetheless excellent for adding interest to any green salad, and it goes famously well with Parmesan cheese and carpaccio (Italian thin-sliced raw beef) or Parma ham. Rocket also makes excellent pesto, in which the de-stalked leaves are pounded in a mortar together with garlic, a little salt and pine kernels. The resulting purée is mixed with fine olive oil and thickened with grated Parmesan to make a superb home-grown sauce for a spring pasta dish.

Rook

Realistically, few of us are ever going to munch on a rook. But the story of their seasonality, together with the fact that it remains theoretically possible for the committed carnivore to get hold of one, makes rooks worth a brief springtime mention. Rooks mate in November and the rookeries in which they live are large, well-organized communities. Anyone who has spent any time very close to a rookery, or parked a car underneath one, will know that they can also be troublesome. Farmers know this most of all: rooks are officially classified as a pest species for the havoc they can play with crops, although they do also eat insect pests. Rookeries are therefore 'thinned' from time to time. Historically this was done by extremely brave and adept tree-climbers who took young rooks by hand; today it is likely to be by shooting. Adult

71

rooks are not good to eat, as the birds are said to become bitter once they are able to fly. It is the young birds (called 'branchers'), having just emerged from their nests for flying practice, that the rook gourmet is after. Their season, usually around May, is brief, because rooks wisely learn to fly quickly.

Only the breasts are worth eating, although the rest can be used for stock. A pie is the traditional home for rook breasts, with more modern treatments of a marinade and barbecue suggested by wildlife chef Hugh Fearnley-Whittingstall in *A Cook on the Wild Side*. Where to get your rook? You will need to know a farmer or landowner who either thins his own or is prepared to let you and your shotgun or air rifle have a go. Or you could visit Shropshire in May, where one butcher (*see p. 156*) briefly stocks rooks if the local populations need controlling that year.

Sorrel

When it arrived in early spring, sorrel was welcomed by our greenery-starved fore-bears. The narrow, pointed leaves are available as early as February and provide a sharp, lemony flavour in the midst of a season when, in the past, nothing else even vaguely fruity or freshly green was available. In *Food for Free*, Richard Mabey notes that the 'plum-skin sharpness' of sorrel was favoured in the Midlands and North of England as a stand-in flavouring in tarts and turnovers between the last stored apples and the first of the season's gooseberries (*see p. 80*). Sorrel occurs widely in the wild, and is best before it flowers in the early summer; it is also cultivated and available for much of the year. Its sharpness is caused by oxalic acid, which its relative rhubarb (*see p. 61*) holds in its leaves in toxic concentrations.

In Britain, sorrel's popularity has waned since the eighteenth century, perhaps due to our progressive conquering of seasonality or, as Jane Grigson suggests in *English Food*, to our obsession with novelty: 'We are so busy running after the latest dish, that the good things we have known for centuries are forgotten as quickly as the boring ones.' It is a useful plant in its season.

> *Things to do with sorrel:* Sorrel pairs well with eggs, which, although no longer seasonal, seem appropriate in spring. Strips can be used to flavour a creamy sauce to be poured over eggs; the leaves can be chopped and added to an omelette, or wilted like spinach to make a comfortable bed for a perfectly poached egg. Sorrel's sharpness works well in soups and stews, and it also suits fish.

June

Treats for the month

June	Seasonal Treats	Coming in	Going out
Vegetables	Beetroot Garlic Peas Turnips	Artichokes, globe Broccoli, calabrese Carrots Cucumber Samphire	Asparagus
Fruit & Nuts	Elderflower Gooseberries	Blackcurrants and redcurrants Cherries Loganberries Raspberries	
Meat, Game & Poultry	Lamb, new season		
Fish & Seafood	Mackerel Sea trout		

June

*'Now summer is in flower and nature's hum
Is never silent round her sultry bloom'*

It's midsummer; but it's not really the middle of the summer. June may contain the longest day of the year, but we have to wait another month or so for the full blast of summer heat, because land and sea warm up more slowly than the air. This time lag is reflected in our seasonal larder: many more things are ready now, but we are still a little way from the peak produce months of August and September. In farming, June is a time for gathering grass, the 'invisible crop' so important to agriculture. This is the time of year when farmers start cutting it and storing it as hay, which is dried grass; or as the more reliable silage, which is grass preserved by fermentation. A good supply is essential to feed livestock through the many months when grass doesn't grow.

Although the seasonal food year has yet to reach its peak, June holds many gourmet delights. Our soft fruit season starts, first with gooseberries, then early raspberries, blackcurrants and cherries. Those looking for a seasonal wild harvest will find elderflower, a perfect companion for gooseberries and the basis of fine summer drinks. Or the gooseberries could be partnered with mackerel, which moves inshore in parts of Britain in the summer months. Wild sea trout, a rare and expensive seasonal fish, is now in prime condition. June also sees the first new-season hill lamb from Wales, to be followed through the summer months by new-season lamb from more northerly and higher places.

Beetroot

Beetroot is hard work. Its earthy, hairy root can take a lot of cooking. Its bright juices stain everything they touch, and can turn the eater's wee a disturbing shade of pink. Beetroot also brings to mind those vinegary discs that emerged from jars to terrorize 1970s salads. It stores well, so is available for much of the year. Why then has it achieved seasonal treat status? Because fresh beetroot is a very good thing; and when the new crop arrives in May or June, it goes excellently with some of the season's other treats: salmon, fresh greens, new potatoes, even, according to food writer Annie Bell, fresh rhubarb.

Small, golfball-sized beetroots have the best flavour. Beetroot is also very good for you, as a source of B vitamins; and it gives you an extra meal from its leaves, which can be eaten like spinach. Beetroot is closely related to chard, which lacks a bulb but has tasty leaves and stems. Its other relatives include mangolds, which are fed to livestock; and sugar beet, from which comes much of the sugar eaten in northern countries. A combination of purple and yellow pigments gives beetroot its striking colour, whose stability makes it an effective dye and thus such a menace in the kitchen.

Preparing beetroot is not complicated. If you want to save your encounter with the dreaded juices until eating time, it is important not to peel or pierce the skin, or pull off the leaves; these should be twisted off. The beetroot can be boiled, although a long, slow roasting – maybe with some garlic alongside – helps its flavour to develop. The skin wrinkles when cooked and will come off easily. Beetroot is magnificent with soured cream, and gives a delicate sweetness to salads.

Elderflower

The flowers of the elder tree are a major contributor to that musky, heady sweetness that can fill the countryside in late spring or early summer. This is partly because the elder is so widespread throughout the British Isles (except in parts of Scotland); partly because the flowers have such a distinctive and pungent fragrance. The flowering can start in May but is most established through June and July. The elder tree itself is surrounded by much folklore: it has been viewed as the 'favourite form for a witch to assume' yet it was also seen as a protection against witchcraft. It also makes excellent pea-shooters, for those given to more light-hearted devilry.

Elderflowers can be cooked and eaten, used to make drinks or to flavour other dishes. For those who have never created food or drink using flowers before, elderflowers are a great place to start, because the results truly are excellent. The simplest way to use the flowers is as a flavouring, in particular for gooseberries, with which elderflower pairs extremely well, in season as well as flavour (*see p. 80*).

Elderflower champagne is a famous use for the flowers, whose natural yeast helps to create a zesty sparkling drink. An admirably minimal recipe from Dorothy Hartley suggests putting freshly gathered heads in a gallon of cold water, stirring in about 500g/1lb of sugar until it is dissolved, then two tablespoons of white wine vinegar and the juice and rind of a lemon. After twenty-four hours in a cool place it is ready to bottle; after two weeks it is ready to drink. In her wine recipe for 'English Frontiniack', eighteenth-century writer Martha Bradley suggests gathering the flowers one or two hours after sunrise, presumably to get them at their most fragrant. The name of this wine is a reference to the ancient and flowery French dessert wine Muscat de Frontignan, whose taste an elderflower wine can approximate. If you'd rather eat the flowers whole, they can be dipped in batter, deep fried and served with a dusting of sugar to create fragrant fritters for pudding. If you're plundering your own elder, though, don't take all the flowers. Spare a thought for the elderberries (*see p. 110*) which provide a second seasonal treat in the autumn.

Garlic

We can, of course, eat garlic all year round, for the garlic we typically eat is of the dried, stored variety. But garlic does have its season, when the fresh (or 'wet') bulb, just harvested, can be eaten as a subtly different delicacy to its more familiar dried counterpart. Garlic is not famous for growing particularly well in Britain; and some foodies consider French varieties to be the only ones worthy of their *aïolis*. Yet grow here it does, to the extent that it even has an Isle of Wight festival in its honour (*see p. 25*). Traditionally, garlic is planted on the shortest day and harvested on the longest, so June is the beginning of the season for wet garlic, which can be had from farmers' markets, vegetable box schemes or good greengrocers.

The fresh stuff is milder, sweeter and less pungent than dried garlic, and good roasted or raw with the season's salads. A pairing of roasted garlic with roasted fresh goat's cheese, ascribed by food writer Annie Bell to Alice Waters of the famous Chez Panisse in California, sounds strange but works magnificently.

Garlic stores well because once exposed to enough summer heat, the bulb goes dormant, ready to push out shoots again in the autumn. Thorough drying – and leaving the long stem intact to reduce shock to the plant – delays this process as long as possible. For this reason, garlic is stored in long plaits of bulbs. Dried garlic is therefore not strictly a seasonal treat. But we should eat as much of it (and its fresh counterpart, when available) as possible, for garlic is good for you. This is something that the British seemed collectively to have forgotten for a few centuries, often associating garlic and its pungency with a suspicious – particularly French – foreignness. The 'basis of good health and good cookery' according to John Seymour, garlic has a range of health benefits including anti-bacterial and anti-fungal qualities; and it acts against the clotting of blood.

Garlic also behaves in interesting ways: the more you crush it, the more pungent it gets. So the terrifying-sounding 'Chicken with 40 cloves of garlic' recipe (*see below*), in which the cloves are used whole and unpeeled, gives but a mild flavouring to the meat, and the cloves can be eaten without fear of bad breath. Crush garlic finely, as you would for *aïoli* (garlic mayonnaise), and people will know what you had for lunch.

Garlic can be pesky to peel: a great tip is to crush the clove with the flat of a knife blade first so the skin just slips off.

Chicken with 40 cloves of garlic

Sounds scary, but the garlic flavours the meat subtly and becomes delicious finger food as well.

1 chicken (the best you can afford)
a small knob of butter
salt and freshly ground black pepper

half a lemon
thyme (optional)
5 heads of garlic
a few tablespoons of olive oil

Preheat the oven to 180°C/350°F/gas 4.

Massage the chicken all over with butter, season with salt and freshly ground pepper, and put it in a roasting tin or large cast-iron pot. Squeeze the lemon over the chicken and put the squeezed lemon in the cavity with some thyme if you have it.

Break up the garlic heads into individual cloves (there's no need to peel them), then scatter them around the chicken. Pour a little olive oil over the garlic, then cover the tray with a double layer of foil (or put on the pot's lid), and put it in the oven for an hour or so.

Remove the foil or lid for a final 15 minutes so that the chicken browns a little; keep an eye on the garlic in case it burns.

Transfer the chicken to a serving plate to rest for at least ten minutes. Scoop out the cloves and keep them warm: they can be squeezed like toothpaste on to slices of French bread, or on to the meat, which will have been delicately perfumed with garlic.

Serves four to six, depending on the size of the chicken.

Gooseberries

Gooseberries are a great yet oft-neglected fruit. Discounting rhubarb (*see p. 61*) which is really a vegetable despite its status as a dessert, gooseberries are the first outdoor fruit of the British year. They share with rhubarb a fresh, tangy astringency that seems an appropriate opener for a berry fruit season whose flavours become sweeter and richer as it progresses through strawberries, raspberries and on to blackberries in the late summer. One of several explanations for the name 'gooseberry' is the fact that its sharp flavour goes well with goose meat: young geese were once eaten at the same time the gooseberry season started (*see p. 111*).

Gooseberry is as celebrated for its relationships as for its own qualities. Its name in France is *groseille à maquereau*, because of its affinity with the mackerel whose season it also partly shares. And the flavour of gooseberries goes very well indeed with elder-flowers (*see p. 78*), which are in full bloom in June: the musky flavour of the flowers improves almost anything you care to make with gooseberries.

Gooseberry is a tough and versatile fruit. It grows well where other fruits don't; all the way up to the Arctic Circle. This has made it popular in Scotland and in the north of England, where, along with many vegetables, gooseberries have become the subject of 'size matters' growing competitions. One such is celebrated every year at Egton Bridge in north Yorkshire (*see p. 25*). For all this, gooseberries are not as popular as they deserve to be. Perhaps it's because some find them too sharp to eat raw, so there is often some effort of preparation involved in gooseberry eating. But it's a small effort, greatly rewarded. Gooseberry fool, for example, simply involves topping and tailing the berries, stewing them gently in butter until soft, then leaving them to cool before folding in an equal amount of whipped double cream and some sugar to taste. Throwing in an elderflower head for flavour while stewing adds to the perfection of this dish.

Both Jane Grigson and Dorothy Hartley float the more complex but interesting tradition of a gooseberry 'raised' pie. Similar in concept to a pork pie, its pastry case is filled with gooseberries, then, after baking, hot apple jelly is poured through a hole in the lid. When cooled and set it can be sliced like a pork pie. Because gooseberries have a short season, it is a happy accident that they also freeze and bottle well so their flavour can reappear all through the year. Margaret Costa's suggestion of making and keeping gooseberry syrup flavoured with elderflower to enhance summer fruit dishes throughout the season seems particularly appealing.

Gooseberry sauce for mackerel: Melt a knob of butter and cook 250g/1/2lb topped and tailed gooseberries until they are soft. Mash them with a fork, and stir in 150ml/1/4 pint double cream, and maybe a pinch of sugar. Serve with a fine fresh mackerel that has been grilled or fried.

Lamb

Lamb is the only widely farmed animal whose consumption retains a seasonal element in Britain. Like almost everything we eat today, it is available all year round: in the case of lamb, antipodean imports have traditionally plugged the December-to-April gap in our own season. The reasons for lamb's seasonality are straightforward: ovulation in ewes is naturally prompted by the shortening days of autumn, so that the birth of lambs, whose gestation period is five months, coincides with the first fresh grass of spring. The term 'lamb' denotes the meat of an animal aged from four months (when it is weaned) to one year old. A bit of basic maths therefore raises the immediate question of why there is a tradition of eating spring lamb at Easter. The answer is marketing: young, sweet lamb is prized in Britain and early supplies can command a premium, so ewes are 'fooled' – with techniques such as hormone impregnation – into breeding earlier.

Lambing happens in the depths of winter and the newest lambs are therefore ready for Easter. Wait a bit later for your new-season lamb, though, and there are more natural rewards to be had. By June, the first new-season 'hill' lamb from Wales starts to hit the shops. This will have had a more relaxed start in life and may well have had time to munch on a bit of real grass and some moorland plants, giving its flesh extra flavour. As the season progresses, new-season lamb from progressively higher and more northerly places arrives in the shops. For example, new-season Herdwick lamb, from a hardy breed raised in the Lake District hills, is not ready until September. So while we may welcome new-season lamb in the late spring, we can continue to enjoy it through the summer and beyond.

As lamb gets older, the meat may lose some of the early pink tenderness and succulence, but it gains in character. And as it ages, it divides gourmets. Some prize the older creatures, 'hoggetts' of one year old or mutton of two years plus. These provide stronger flavours and tougher meat, and mutton – once a major feature of the British diet – is making a comeback, with specialist producers feeding the appetites of connoisseurs.

Lamb is versatile and easy to prepare; its fattiness means a sharp accompaniment is always a good idea. Shoulder is cheaper than leg, fattier but somehow more succulent. The supposed complexity of carving it means it is often sold boned and rolled: easier, however, just to sit the shoulder on some halved heads of garlic and stalky rosemary, and let a hot oven do the rest. The carving is fun, and crabapple jelly makes a fine, if unseasonal, accompaniment if you're bored with mint sauce. Otherwise, the season offers such perfect vegetable partners as new potatoes, carrots and peas.

Mackerel

As a gastronomic treat, mackerel have everything going for them. They are utterly beautiful to look at, excellent eating, easy to catch and clean (should you be that way inclined), very good for you and, unusually for fish, cheap to buy. So it's strange that they are not more popular in this country. Perhaps it's their reputation as a carnivorous scavenger, which seems entirely undeserved, as many fish are carnivorous, and mackerel concentrate on crustaceans and smaller fish. Or maybe it's the fact that they spoil easily. Freshness is vitally important in mackerel if you are to avoid an unpleasantly woolly dish: for this reason, mackerel used to be sold on Sundays, even in Scotland. Or it could be their oiliness: fish such as mackerel and herring (also underused as a fresh fish) need a well-ventilated kitchen if they are being grilled or fried.

None of these reasons outweighs the many justifications for seeking out mackerel, which are available all year round but move inshore and north in the summer months, the traditional time for eating them. They are rich in long-chain omega 3 polyunsaturated fatty acids, which are a bit of a mouthful but terrifically good for you. These substances, more or less uniquely sourced from oil-rich fish, are implicated in boosting brain power, fighting coronary disease and reducing blood pressure.

Mackerel are also one of the few fish that the completely amateur, hopelessly equipped sea angler has a chance of catching. Shiny spinners or feathered hooks towed behind a dinghy, or cast into a propitious spot, stand a good chance of hauling one (or a few) in. Then, of course, you have the ultimate mackerel treat of preparing yourself the freshest fish available. Otherwise, mackerel are easy to get hold of in good fishmongers; they are oilier in the winter, when they tend to be trawler-caught. They are also caught by a hand-line fleet of smaller boats in the South-west of England, a fishery that offers both sustainability and employment in local communities.

What to do with them? Grilled or fried, with a bay leaf and some lemon involved somewhere, they are excellent. Bigger fish can be baked. The sharpness of gooseberry or rhubarb sauce cuts the oiliness well and is seasonally in tune with the fish (*see p. 81 for the gooseberry sauce recipe*). Or, if you're satisfied the fish is as fresh as it can be, you could take the minimal, no-cooking approach: mackerel sashimi is fantastic. Finally, it's also worth seeking out hot-smoked mackerel for its delightful taste and texture as well as for the promise of fine pâté.

Peas

There are some to whom the concept of a season for peas is utterly irrelevant. Peas are one of the very few food items whose frozen version can be better than the fresh. There's a simple reason for this. The sugars in peas start converting to starch as soon as they are picked, so quality diminishes fast. Freezing, which for commercially grown peas is done within 2½ hours of picking, stops this process dead in its tracks, so frozen peas are not bad at all. Unless you can be absolutely sure that the fresh peas you have bought in season, snug in their pods, have come straight off the vine, then chances are the frozen version would be better eating. Does this mean we should forget about fresh peas? Of course not. If you have access to a really good supplier, or grow them yourself, fresh peas are a delight during the summer months.

Peas in Britain have a long, important history. The grey or 'field' pea was a major staple food through the Middle Ages, when it was widely grown for its great food value and for the fact that it dried well to provide vital nutrition through the winter. A world away from the glamour of a zingy fresh garden pea, the field pea was a key ingredient of pease pottage, a staple soup; and later of pease pudding, in which the peas are wrapped in a cloth and boiled alongside some bacon to create a solid, round, allegedly tasty pudding. Such was the importance of the medieval pea harvest that a height limit was imposed on the vines so they could not provide shelter for unscrupulous pea-thieves. Today's garden pea was not introduced until the sixteenth century, when it began as a luxury import before being more widely cultivated. It was an early candidate for canning, but tinned peas are often dyed to restore their greenness. The frozen pea industry won out in the UK, and now produces more peas for freezing than any other European country.

Truly fresh garden peas, though, have a flavour that not even the frozen version can match. When ready, the pods should be bright green, and juicy when they open. Raw, they add a tasty green bite to salads; cooked, they are delicious on their own or with little more than butter and chopped mint. They also make excellent soups and a fine summer risotto, and go famously well with bacon and ham. A pairing with duck was traditional in early June.

If you're getting into serious edible gardening, peas (part of the legume family) form an important part of a crop rotation. Their root nodules release atmospheric nitrogen into the soil, creating fertile conditions for brassicas such as cabbages and broccoli. And if you grow too many peas, you can quickly blanch and freeze your own, giving you the best of both pea worlds.

Sea trout

Like wild salmon, from which they can be difficult to distinguish, sea trout does not have a happy recent history. They are a popular game fish for their large size and eating quality, yet other factors are behind the sharp decline in their populations from the late 1980s onwards. Sea trout are said to have been badly affected by the sea lice associated with salmon farming; steps are being taken to address this issue, but climate change may also be affecting the life cycles of sea trout and other migratory, seasonal fish (*see also salmon, eels, elvers, pp. 62, 124 and 50*). Sea trout are biologically indistinguishable from brown trout, the main difference being that brown trout choose (wisely, it would appear) not to migrate to the sea, but remain a freshwater game fish, also highly esteemed for their eating quality but not in the same league as sea trout. The sea trout's life cycle is similar to salmon's, in that they grow in fresh water before migrating to the sea, then head back to freshwater rivers to spawn. It is at this point that they are the gourmet's target: returning sea trout are fat and extra-tasty, the crustaceans in their diet having given their flesh a similar pink colour to salmon's.

In the summer, as they return to spawn, sea trout, like wild salmon, are a rare and wonderful delicacy. The ethical dilemma remains, though: should one eat them? The answer is not straightforward, but would we care about – or have noticed – the crash in stocks if sea trout weren't so prized for sport? Many creatures thrive in the wild today only because they are managed – to varying degrees – by man (*see grouse, p. 124*). If maintaining its status as a luxurious delicacy is a way of assuring the sea trout's survival in the face of man's more systematic attacks on its habitats and lifestyle, then it seems worth doing.

Turnips

Turnips have a rather grim association in Britain with animal fodder and poverty. This is not unjustified, for they have a significant place in British agricultural history. Championed by Viscount Charles 'Turnip' Townshend in the eighteenth century, turnips were a key part of the 'Norfolk four-course' crop rotation that helped to keep the soil in good condition. Crucially, they gave livestock something to eat over the winter so we could keep more cattle. Turnips, in essence, helped to protect us from the seasons. Today turnips retain their earthy reputation, reinforced in part by their central position in the diet of Baldrick, the grubby retainer in the *Blackadder* television series. For the French, who revere many foods that the British distrust, turnips are a vegetable of glamour and delicacy, reflected in their elegant name, *navet*.

Turnips do appear as an autumn/winter crop – and some of these later plants still end up nourishing cattle – but the earlier, smaller summer turnips are the ones of interest for the seasonal gourmet. They have an excellent flavour and can be braised, or chopped and glazed with sugar, or just boiled until tender. Margaret Costa in the *Four Seasons Cookery Book* suggests pairings with duck and roast lamb.

Turnip tops, the leaves of the plant, are also good eating and make a fine alternative to spring greens. Turnip is closely related to rape, whose yellow flowers are now a major fixture of the British agricultural year. *Cime di rapa* is a related Italian delicacy with a more fashionable-sounding name than turnip tops. A final word on turnips: when the Scots talk of 'neeps', they mean the orange-fleshed swede (*see p. 33*), a close relative.

July

Treats for the month

July	Seasonal Treats	Coming in	Going out
Vegetables	Artichokes, globe Beans, broad Cucumber	Beans, French Beans, runner Fennel Kohlrabi Shallots	
Fruit & Nuts	Blackcurrants and redcurrants Blueberries Cherries Strawberries		Elderflower
Meat, Game & Poultry			
Fish & Seafood	Lobster		

July

'Daughter of pastoral smells and sights
And sultry days and dewy nights'

July brings summer in its full intensity. With luck, we should have the warmest, most settled weather of the year, perfect for the crops and produce that are shortly to be harvested. Fields of wheat, barley and oats will be starting to take on their ripe yellow colour. The tricky business of haymaking continues. And with widespread flowering of grasses and plants throughout the countryside, July is a terrible time for hayfever sufferers but a great month for butterflies and their enthusiasts.

On the food front, this month's seasonal specialities match the weather perfectly. June's selection of fine berry fruits is joined by strawberries and blueberries, making July the perfect time for a lazy day at the pick-your-own followed by the construction of summer pudding. It's also the very beginning of the English apple season, with early varieties such as Beauty of Bath and George Cave coming in towards the end of the month. An old saying warns against premature scrumping, though: 'Till St Swithin's day [15 July] be past, apples be not fit to taste.'

In the garden and the greengrocer's, the range of seasonal produce is growing rapidly now. French beans and runner beans are ready to accompany a succulent roast of new-season hill lamb. Globe artichoke plants will be looking magnificent, but it's time to hack off their heads and eat them. Fennel arrives to flavour summer fish dishes. And lobster should be more easily (if expensively) available to form the centrepiece of a summer feast.

Artichokes, globe

Globe artichokes can cause serious embarrassment. It's not their after-effects (they mercifully don't share those of their unrelated Jerusalem namesakes); rather it's the fact that artichoke novices may not know quite what to do with them. On my artichoke début, I was allowed grimly to chew and swallow quite a few of the leaves before a mischievous host pointed out that one should simply scrape off the soft flesh with one's teeth before depositing the tough leaves in the bowl provided. Once you've got the hang of this, it is, of course, merely a tantalizing prelude to the artichoke heart, which, when you've discarded the nasty hairy 'choke', is the real reason for going to the leafy trouble of eating one. The hearts are soft, tender and delicately flavoured.

Gardening expert Monty Don considers globe artichokes to be 'the handsomest of all edible plants', so if (as I do) you want pretty much everything in the garden to be edible, they will please the aesthetes as well as the gourmets. The part that is eaten is, in fact, an immature flower head that looks even more spectacular when allowed to bloom. British artichokes are not widely available; but July is a good time to seek them out in farmers' markets or maybe take them from your own garden.

There's little point in hunting out recipes for globe artichokes. They simply need to be boiled until the leaves (or bracts, to give them their proper name) come off easily: use tongs, rather than fingers, to test for this. Thereafter, melted butter, perhaps herb-flavoured, makes a good dipping sauce. Like any food that involves the eater in a bit of manual labour, artichokes make a convivial dinner-party dish, as long as you make sure everyone knows what to do.

Beans, broad

Broad beans have a season which is either short or medium-sized, depending on how you like your beans. When the pods are small and tender, around May, they can be eaten whole; shortly thereafter the beans within can be prepared and eaten like peas, and are equally delicious. Around June they were traditionally eaten as an accompaniment to a young duck. As the season progresses, the beans get tougher, needing longer, slower cooking: late-summer broad beans will need to be skinned to reveal the tender, bright-green bean within. And at the end of the season the mature, wrinkled bean is really only good for drying or making into hearty soups. In a way, the culinary applications of a broad bean suit the progression of the seasons, but the earlier, fresher eating is worth seeking out. The non-gardeners among us will, however, have to content ourselves with the tougher beans, as this is how fresh broad beans are often sold. These are good for braises and risottos, or garlicky purées.

The gardeners not only get to pick the young, tender beans; they also have the pleasure of the plant's tops, which are a delicacy in their own right. Broad beans share with their pea relatives (*see p. 83*) a rapid deterioration once picked, so freshness really is key. A garden glut can be successfully blanched and frozen to avoid an excess of tough, end-of-season beans. These can, however, be dried, whereafter they are useful in hearty winter dishes, the most extreme of which must be a dish of bacon and beans recalled by Dorothy Hartley. A ham hock is placed with dried beans, honey, water and seasonings in a large, almost-sealed jar and baked for around twenty-four hours. One for Aga owners, perhaps.

In the *Oxford Companion to Food*, Alan Davidson notes that in Greek, Roman and Celtic societies, broad beans had associations with the dead; and that this may relate to a rare condition called favism in which susceptible consumers are stricken with severe anaemia and jaundice. One wonders whether it was this dark reputation that prompted Hannibal Lecter to choose broad beans to accompany his liver and Chianti in *The Silence of the Lambs*. None of this should put us off broad beans, though: they are a versatile, nutritious treat that changes through their season.

Blackcurrants and redcurrants

The appearance of blackcurrants and redcurrants in July means that the British summer fruit season is really getting into its stride. Arriving a little later than their relative the gooseberry (*see p. 80*), blackcurrants and redcurrants bring interesting possibilities for the seasonal gourmet, most notably the first decent summer pudding of the year (*see recipe overleaf*). Which currant you prefer is a matter of taste; each has its own merits. Both types grow well in cool, northern climates and thus have never caught on gastronomically in the gourmet states of the Mediterranean as they have in Britain.

Redcurrants were the first to be cultivated, esteemed above blackcurrants which were shunned for their smelly leaves. Redcurrants make an excellent jelly to accompany fatty meats such as lamb, and their high pectin content makes them a useful partner in jam-making for lower-pectin fruits such as blackberries, rhubarb or pears.

Blackcurrants were a medicine before they became a dessert; the juice was used for soothing sore throats and the leaves can improve tea. However, the discovery that they are extremely rich in vitamin C led to the blackcurrant's position today as a hugely popular ingredient for cordials, commercial varieties of which use 95 per cent of Britain's blackcurrant harvest. There are more interesting things to do with blackcurrants than making soft drinks, however: their vitamin-packed goodness can be more convivially appreciated in the medium of *crème de cassis*, the basis of a good *kir* or *kir royale*. Blackcurrants are good raw, particularly in summer pudding, and also make fine jams, jellies, ice creams and sorbets. Like any British summer fruit, they are best eaten in season and as fresh as possible, so growing or picking your own is always a good option.

Blackcurrant growing has a long history in the west Midlands, particularly Herefordshire; but climate change puts a question mark over how long this will continue. Together with other fruit crops, blackcurrants need a period of cold-induced dormancy in order for buds – and thus flowers and fruit – to develop. If less cold-dependent varieties are not developed before the climate warms, production may be forced northwards.

Summer pudding

A classic, delicious seasonal dessert and the perfect thing to do with summer berry fruits. It needs to be made in advance, though.

1kg/2lb berry fruit (blackcurrants, blueberries,
raspberries, redcurrants, blackberries)
250g/8oz sugar
day-old good white bread, crusts removed

Put the fruit into a bowl with the sugar, and leave overnight. The next day transfer the fruit and sugar into a pan, bring to the boil and simmer for a few minutes only.

Cut thin slices of bread to line a 900ml/1^1/2 pint pudding basin: a circular piece for the base, and wedge-shaped pieces for the sides. Pour in half the fruit and juice, add a slice of bread, then pour in the rest. Top with a couple of layers of bread, trimming them to fit the bowl neatly. Put a saucer on top, weight it, and leave overnight (or longer) in the fridge.

When you want to eat the pudding, remove the saucer and weight, place a serving plate upside down over the pudding, and invert the plate and bowl quickly. Removing the basin should reveal a beautiful pudding whose bread case is saturated with syrupy fruit juices. Serve with plenty of cream.
Good for six to eight people.

Blueberries

Blueberries have a short history in Britain, having been grown here commercially only since the 1930s. Their relative the bilberry (or blaeberry or whortleberry) grows wild throughout most of the country; in Ireland it was associated with a festival of both picking and courting at the end of July. Bilberries are hard to pick in any quantity, but famed for making excellent tarts. Those unwilling to go to the considerable trouble of picking could at least enjoy bilberries' influence in the early autumn; they may form part of the diet of Herdwick lambs (*see p. 82*), ready for eating by September.

The fame of the blueberry, however, seems set to spread as attention has recently focused on its health-giving properties. Blueberries are rich in antioxidants and, along with other berries, were credited with reversing short-term memory loss in a 1999 study quoted by the *Journal of Neuroscience*. So perhaps they are a seasonal treat to which the children of the 1960s should pay particular attention. The brevity of the British culinary repertoire matches blueberries' short history; like bilberries, they are excellent in pies and tarts. Blueberries are suited to making muffins because they explode within the muffin mix while it cooks, spreading their flavour about the place; this also works with pancakes. And like all berry fruits, they are perfect in a summer pudding (*see above*).

Cherries

Cherries are a fickle feature of the British fruit year. Peaking in July, their season is short; and they are highly susceptible to our unpredictable weather, with yields varying greatly from one year to another. Together with the insistence of the few retailers who now dominate our food chain on metronomic predictability and consistency, this capriciousness has not worked in British cherries' favour. The acreage under cultivation has declined to such an extent that the tonnage of imports now exceeds the home-grown crop by a factor of more than ten. Will we continue to see British cherries? Not in many supermarkets, who take only 20 per cent of the home-grown crop: if you want a fine in-season British cherry, better to visit the greengrocer, farmers' market, roadside stall or pick-your-own. Imported fruit is said by some to be superior, and southern European cherries certainly have a longer season; but there's a special joy in catching our own crop at its brief best, safe in the knowledge that it hasn't spent too long on the road.

British cherries' arrival coincides neatly with some of our other summer fruits, ready to fill a lovely bowl of seasonal fresh fruit and berries. The vast majority of British cherries are grown in Kent, with Worcestershire the northern limit of commercial cultivation, so the South-east is the best place to find the growers. Despite their short-lived season, it seems fitting to make the most of cherries when they are at their prime and ignore them for the rest of the year: a bowl of cherries would be incongruous at, say, an autumn dinner table. Preparing them seems irrelevant, because little can be done to improve on the sweet/tart flavour of a good, ripe cherry. Adding them to a summer pudding (*see p. 92*) is one possibility. Investing in a cherry stoner is not a bad idea, either. One of a few 'labour-saving' kitchen devices worth having, it will also de-stone your olives.

Cucumber

Cucumbers have been cultivated for over 3,000 years. Why? They are 96 per cent water and have virtually no nutritional value. To my mind it is an indicator of the leisure of ancient societies that they could devote so much energy to a vegetable that provided so little. Cucumbers, along with their relative the melon, originate in Africa and Asia and thus like things to be a little warmer than Britain can manage. As a result, many are grown under glass; but hardier, 'ridge' cucumbers, with ugly, spiny skins but a finer flavour, do grow outdoors here. July is the earliest that these are likely to appear; the further south you are, the more likely your craving for an early-ish outdoor cucumber is to be satisfied.

It seems worthwhile seeking out the most 'artisanal' cucumber you can find, because the dead straight, inch-perfect glasshouse varieties available all year round are pretty bland; and for a vegetable that's bland anyway, that's bad. There is something about its subtle, refreshing flavour, though, that earns the cucumber its place in the genteel sandwiches and Pimm's glasses of summer. Chopped and mixed with plain yoghurt to make *raita*, it's more refreshing still. Just the thing for a hot curry or a hot summer's day.

Lobster

There are a couple of reasons for lobster's position as a summer dish. They get livelier as the water warms, and move into shallower water where they are easier to get hold of. In winter, the cold water slows them down and makes them less inclined to clamber into a pot. Then there's the more prosaic fact that going out in a tiny boat to pull up lobster pots in wild winter seas is not a particularly tempting prospect, even for hard-as-nails Scottish fishermen. So summer is the best time for lobster.

Like pretty much everything in the sea that's good to eat these days, lobster is depleted in numbers; it's also unlikely to reach the great age (up to fifty years) and impressive dimensions (up to a metre long and 20kg) of which it is capable. Lobster is in great demand, having been considered a gourmet food since the nineteenth century. In continental Europe, where seafood is taken very seriously, British – in particular Scottish – lobsters are much sought after. A few years ago I was shocked to see two vast lorries from northern Spain picking up lobsters from the slipway to the Iona ferry on the island of Mull. It's a long way to drive for a few crustaceans, and testimony both to the demand and the esteem in which they are held by our neighbours. It also explains why they can be hard to get hold of in their native country.

Moves are afoot now to conserve UK stocks: a practice called 'v-notching' (cutting a notch in the lobster's tail that takes two years to grow out) identifies egg-bearing females that should be left to release their young and grow. The legal minimum size for a lobster to be eaten is a carapace length of 87mm. There are also hatcheries in Cornwall, Orkney and Anglesey to bolster wild stocks. All of this means lobster is an expensive delicacy; and rightly so. It makes for a ceremonial meal and its rich, succulent tail meat lends itself to decadent sauces.

Cooking lobster: The big lobster issue, particularly for the creature itself, is how to kill it. To guarantee freshness, a lobster should ideally be purchased live, when its exoskeleton is a speckled blue-black (cooking releases a red pigment which gives it the characteristic pink colour). This means the cook has to deliver the coup de grâce. Because lobsters don't have anything much resembling a brain, a knock to the head won't finish them off. How then to dispatch them? Serious chefs tend just to hurl them into boiling water or start hacking at them straight away. It is said to be kinder to put them in cold salt water so that they expire more peacefully as the water warms up; and kinder still to freeze them at −18°C for two hours so that they fall asleep before giving up the ghost. Whichever way you choose, a fine summer delicacy awaits. The easiest way to cook a lobster is simply to boil it in sea water (or water with enough salt added to keep an egg floating) for 15 minutes for the first 1/2kg/1lb, then ten minutes for each subsequent 1/2kg.

Strawberries

We may not be able to grow citrus or exotic fruits particularly well in Britain, but our climate is perfect for berry fruits and stone fruits. And of all the berry fruits that evoke the seasons, strawberries must top the list (particularly in England) for their association with languid afternoons in early summer. So what are strawberries doing on the shelves in December, then? Getting in the way of other stuff, that's what. Strawberries really are best in their season. They don't keep when ripe and damage incredibly easily, so imported ones will have been picked early for ease of transport and ripened artificially with ethylene gas. British glasshouse strawberries now start in April and extend the season right through until December, and although they won't have had to travel too far, they are unlikely to have seen the warm, direct sunlight that makes a just-picked, in-season strawberry such a delight.

The proper strawberry season starts in June, and a range of different varieties means that outdoor strawberries can keep going until early autumn. That said, around 80 per cent of in-season supermarket strawberries are of one variety, Elsanta, chosen for its appearance, shelf life and flavour. Supermarket strawberries will be OK in season, although they will have been picked before ripeness and chilled for the inevitable journey from grower to distribution hub to shop. Seekers after the optimum strawberry experience should grow their own or head for a local supplier or pick-your-own farm, where the fruit can be picked ripe and eaten soon afterwards. Refrigeration does not improve strawberries; they're nicest eaten at (summer) room temperature.

Small, fragrant wild strawberries can be found from late June until August in woods and scrubland, and are a pleasant surprise if you find them. A similar variety, named Alpine, can easily be grown to create a more reliable supply of this delicate fruit.

Advice on preparing strawberries seems utterly irrelevant. As long as they are fresh and ripe, why go further than the best cream you can afford and as much sugar as you will allow yourself?

August

Treats for the month

August	Seasonal Treats	Coming in	Going out
Vegetables	Aubergine Beans, French Beans, runner Broccoli, Courgettes, Fennel, Samphire	Leeks Mushrooms, wild Squash and pumpkins Sweetcorn Tomatoes	Radishes Shallots
Fruit & Nuts	Cobnuts	Apples Blackberries Pears Plums	Cherries
Meat, Game & Poultry		Grouse	
Fish & Seafood			Salmon, wild

August

'Harvest approaches with its bustling day
The wheat tans brown and barley bleaches grey'

For most of us, August is a month to take it easy, go away, or generally idle in the summer heat. For many farmers, it's time for the most important harvest of the year: holidays are not an option. The gathering in of cereal crops such as wheat, barley and oats is highly seasonal, and these foods are central to our diet. Yet because they store well and are processed into so many different things, we don't think of them as seasonal foods, so the most important harvest (Britain remains largely self-sufficient in wheat, for example) can go completely unnoticed by all except country dwellers. The harvest was once celebrated as Lughnasadh or Lammas (from the Saxon, meaning 'loaf festival'), originally one of the four Celtic festivals that mark key points in the natural and farming cycle.

Cereals are not the only things harvested in August: the month offers a huge array of fresh, in-season produce. Vegetables that need more heat to mature – such as aubergines, courgettes and tomatoes – are now ready, so this is a good month for making ratatouille. The growing array of British fruit is joined by pears, plums and blackberries, with cobnuts providing the season's first fresh nuts. The countryside as a whole may be starting to look a little tired as the summer's greenness fades: and as a further reminder of oncoming autumn, the game season opens with a bang on 12 August: ptarmigan, snipe and, most significantly, grouse are in the firing line.

Aubergine

Aubergines occupy a tenuous place in the British seasonal vegetable garden, preferring things to be warmer and more humid than they tend to be in Britain. The status of the aubergine is much greater in Mediterranean climates, where it is the foundation of such famous dishes as moussaka (Greece), and *baba ghanoush* and *imam bayildi* in the eastern Mediterranean and the Arab world. The aubergine's original introduction in Europe was subject to the suspicion that seems always to have greeted members of the nightshade family to which it belongs. Its Italian name, *melanzana*, is derived from the Latin meaning 'apple of madness'; and its relatives the tomato and potato were ascribed similarly unwelcome properties before being accepted as culinary staples. In Britain, the aubergine was originally cultivated as a decorative plant, with small white fruits (like the tomato, the aubergine is classed as a fruit but used as a vegetable) that gave it the alternative name of 'eggplant'.

The aubergine's British season is quite short. It needs the greatest heat of our summer in order to thrive outdoors, so August is the time to start looking for British aubergines that have benefited from a bit of sun; glasshouse aubergines can be bland.

Aubergines are very useful in the late-summer kitchen. They arrive at the same time as courgettes and tomatoes, setting things up perfectly for ratatouille (*see recipe*), which is a great staple of late-summer meals and barbecues. Aubergines can also be slapped on to the barbecue themselves and char-grilled for the vegetarians or to start off a *baba ghanoush* (in which the grilled aubergines are puréed with yoghurt, garlic and lemon). They are famous for demanding vast quantities of oil, and most cooks suggest resisting the temptation to feed their habit, as the juices will eventually run out to help the frying process.

Whether to salt and press them before cooking? It's a matter of preference. Contemporary varieties are said to have had bred out of them the bitterness that this process is designed to correct, so many question the value of doing it. I like the routine of weighting a big colander full of chopped aubergines and courgettes, and am convinced that the end result is a better ratatouille.

Ratatouille

A superb, versatile dish that makes the most of the seasonal collision of tomatoes, aubergines and courgettes. It is worth making in advance, because it improves with time. There are countless methods of preparation: this is mine.

1 large aubergine (or 2 small ones), roughly chopped
3–4 courgettes, roughly chopped
salt
2–3 medium onions, chopped
6 cloves garlic, chopped
extra virgin olive oil

500g/1lb tomatoes (the freshest you can lay your hands on)
2 bay leaves
sprig of thyme
a good slug of red wine
salt and freshly ground black pepper
Tabasco

Put the chopped aubergine and courgettes in a colander, salting as you go, and weight them with a small plate and something heavy for an hour.

Cook the onions and garlic gently in copious quantities of extra virgin olive oil, in a large, heavy-bottomed pan. Stir occasionally (or sprinkle with a little salt) to prevent the onions browning: you want them soft and sweet but not caramelized.

While the onions are cooking, put the tomatoes into a bowl and pour boiling water over them. After a few minutes, pour off the water and slip off the tomato skins. Quarter them, removing the seeds and cores.

The onions should now be done. Rinse the courgettes and aubergines, dry them with a tea towel and stir them into the onions. Put on a lid, and cook on a low heat until all is soft. Then add the tomatoes, two bay leaves and a good sprig of thyme (tied up for tidiness if you prefer), a slug of red wine, many grindings of black pepper and a little salt and Tabasco. Bring to the boil and simmer for 30 minutes.

Refrigerate it for a day once cooled, if you can wait that long. Ratatouille goes particularly well with chicken with 40 cloves of garlic (*see p. 80*). *Serves four.*

Beans, French (green beans, haricots verts)

How better to kick back against the madness of the globalized food market than by buying British-grown French beans in season? French beans (or green beans, or haricots verts) are conspicuously available all year round, often flown in from Kenya, ready topped and tailed, and packaged to within an inch of their lives. If you care about the taste of a vegetable whose eating quality declines from the minute it is taken off the plant, then buying fresh green beans grown around 4,000 miles away seems crazy enough. If you also care about the quantities of untaxed aviation fuel burned in order to get them to our supermarkets, it seems crazier still. With a huge range of tasty, in-season British veg fighting for our attention outside the brief window in which French beans grow in Britain, why does such perversity persist? It's a long and complex story, to do with marketing, profit margins and the elimination of risk. It doesn't, however, have much to do with gastronomy, despite what its proponents would have us believe.

French beans are not a British staple, probably because they prefer things to be slightly warmer than our climate routinely manages; so the hardier broad bean and the runner bean (*see pp. 90 and 102*) have a more significant history in our country. They are, however, excellent eating and they do grow here, with a season that begins in July and extends into October. Getting hold of the British item can be tricky outside of farmers' markets, so growing your own – which is relatively easy, decorative, and deliciously seasonal – may be the best option. French beans are good cooked and then left to cool; however, in my view there is only one thing to do with them: briefly boiled until tender, and then sautéed gently in garlic and butter, they are the perfect accompaniment to a rare steak, which, at this time of year, might have come straight off a barbecue.

Beans, runner

It's hard to write about runner beans with passion. They can be tender, tasty and a delightful addition to a late-summer dinner; or they can be stringy and nasty, better as dental floss than as a vegetable side dish. Perhaps the memory of the bad ones blots out the reality that runner beans can be a fine summer vegetable.

So named because of their fondness for climbing, runner beans are thought to have come from Mexico, where they grow at some altitude. Their original function in Britain was decorative: the climbing runner-bean plant with abundant bright (often red) flowers lights up gardens and allotments in July and August. Like many other vegetables beloved of allotment gardeners, runner beans are the subject of competitive growing; sadly for the gourmet, these competitions tend to be for size rather than eating quality. Perhaps as a legacy of the vegetable show, we in Britain are unique in the masochism of eating runner beans when they are long and stringy. Better to catch them early, say at 15cm/6 inches or less, when they are more tender.

As with other legumes such as peas, the sugars in runner beans convert to starch after picking, so freshness is crucially important if they are to be worth the bother. Growing your own is not difficult, and constant picking can provide a fresh supply that lasts until the first big frosts. In a nod to the sensitive gourmets among us who shun the stringiest runners, self-sufficiency expert John Seymour suggests throwing any excess to the pigs. Those of us not blessed with a pair of pigs can use the medium of chutney to deal with a glut of runner beans.

British runner beans are easy to get hold of in their season, but be sure to seek out the freshest-looking pods. Preparation is simple, although the task of slicing is improved by a bean slicer, which can be anything from a hand-cranked gadget to a mesh of blades through which the pods are pushed. Fine slicing means they cook more evenly. Runner beans sliced and briefly boiled are a worthy partner to the other meat and veg of a Sunday roast, where they will happily help mop up good gravy.

Broccoli (calabrese)

The broccoli that we see the most of is also known as calabrese, after the Italian region from which it originates. Its British season is summer and autumn, although it is imported and widely available throughout the year. Calabrese suffers from being overshadowed by more glamorous relatives: purple sprouting broccoli (see p. 50), a major, short-lived seasonal treat of the early spring; and romanesco, an autumn variety, more visually appealing with its extraordinarily patterned bright green heads.

Despite this, calabrese merits our attention. Even more than its goodness-packed brassica relatives such as cabbages and Brussels sprouts, broccoli in general is famed for its nutritional value. It is rich in vitamins, antioxidants and compounds thought to fight cancer. However, most of these are destroyed if broccoli is given the old-fashioned British overboiling treatment, or blasted in a microwave oven. Which is another good reason for avoiding overcooked broccoli: the main reason is, of course, that it is ghastly.

Treat calabrese with the respect its payload of goodness deserves, though, and it is a delight. The 'florets' of broccoli (from the Italian for 'little shoots') are in fact made up of tightly packed, unopened flower buds and form the tastiest and most delicate part of the plant. A brief steaming is the best way to prepare them while still retaining the nutrients; once tender, they work surprisingly well stirred into pasta dishes as well as taking their traditional place as a vegetable side dish. The rest of the plant need not be discarded. The leaves can be steamed like greens, and the thick stalks either added to stock or chopped up small and steamed alongside the florets. Broccoli's eating quality and nutritional value deteriorate rapidly, so it should be acquired as close to its source as possible and eaten soon after purchase.

Cobnuts

Enjoying the seasonal treat of a cobnut means being in the right place at the right time. Cobnuts, also known as filberts, are cultivated hazelnuts and the centre of their growing in Britain is Kent, with Kentish Cob the most common variety grown. The season for the nuts, which are sold fresh, is relatively short, starting in mid-August and continuing until October. Cobnut production declined sharply in the twentieth century, partly because maintaining the orchards is labour-intensive. As with many local, seasonal British delicacies, there is renewed interest in cobnuts, which have an association dedicated to their promotion. As yet, however, cobnuts are not distributed widely outside the areas in which they are grown (which also include Sussex, Devon and Worcestershire) so they remain largely a seasonal treat for southerners.

Different to the more familiar dried hazelnut, fresh cobnuts have a crunchy texture and milky flavour that develop as the season progresses. Should you wish to grow your own cobnuts, the tree is a fine thing but you will be at war with squirrels. As Hugh Fearnley-Whittingstall says of finding wild hazelnuts in *The River Cottage Cookbook*: 'If you want to find a hazel tree, follow a squirrel. And if you want to get a decent crop of nuts off it, shoot the squirrel.'

Courgettes

Courgettes have a very short history as a British seasonal vegetable. They are, in essence, a small marrow, the growing of which to prodigious sizes has featured in our vegetable culture for a little longer. Few will have happy childhood memories of fine marrow feasts, though; while they may look impressive, giant marrows are bland and good only as a vehicle for other flavours. In the gourmet's garden, they are a waste of space. Courgettes, on the other hand, have a great deal more gastronomic merit. The Italians, who gave them their other common name, *zucchini*, were the first to popularize their eating. The courgette's introduction into the British gastronomic canon is ascribed by *Oxford Companion to Food* author Alan Davidson to Elizabeth David, who did so much to promote Mediterranean food in this country.

Courgettes grow well here, with a British season that peaks in the heat of August;

and as they fade away in the autumn, their thicker-skinned relatives pumpkins and winter squashes take over. Amateur vegetable growers with a little bit of space might want to add courgettes to their outdoor larder. They provide a good harvest, because they keep producing if you cut the courgettes before they mature to marrow size. Courgettes grow both male and female flowers: the females mature into courgettes while the males just look pretty then fall off.

There are far too many ways with the versatile courgette to list here. It is a key ingredient of ratatouille (*see p. 100*), delicious on its own steamed, or sautéed gently in olive oil. Very small courgettes can be sliced and eaten raw in salads. The flowers are also part of the courgette-eating experience. In the event that you find courgettes on sale with the flowers attached, their condition is a good indicator of how fresh the vegetable is. If you grow your own, then the non-productive male flowers can be used as well: stuffing them is a popular solution, maybe with a mixture based on cheese and cream. They can then be battered and deep-fried. Sounds like a good British idea, but it is in fact Italian.

Courgettes don't keep well, a good reason for eating them in season or growing your own; and they are 90 per cent water, so – in the unlikely event you can resist the temptation to prepare them with vast amounts of fine olive oil – they won't make you fat.

Fennel

As an import from a warmer country – Italy – fennel needs the strength of the British summer in order to mature here, although too much heat is bad for it. The British fennel season therefore picks up when the Italian one ends, with our own crop in the shops from July until the autumn. Fennel does seem a little exotic and foreign, its aniseed flavour evocative of Mediterranean fish dishes and not to everyone's taste. It fits neatly into the produce season in Britain, however. The stalks and fronds of Florence fennel, which, with its fat bulb, is the most common culinary variety, are excellent in stock, particularly that which is destined to accompany fish. The bulb itself, which is in fact a tight bunch of overlapping leaf stems, is much more versatile than it might seem when it first meets you in the kitchen, defying you to think what could possibly be done with it.

> *Things to do with fennel:* Sliced very thinly, fennel can be eaten raw and added to salads, where its singular flavour provides interest. A peppy side dish can be had by combining sliced raw fennel with shaved Parmesan cheese and balsamic vinegar. Next easiest is to slice it more thickly and char-grill it, serving the fennel with lemon juice and olive oil. It cooks well, particularly when braised with a little stock. It also roasts well if blanched first for a couple of minutes. Food writer Annie Bell suggests a fennel *brandade*, in which several bulbs are cooked with thyme and garlic then liquidized with olive oil before being mixed with mashed new potatoes. A scattering of samphire, which shares much of fennel's season, completes the dish.

Samphire

'Rock or marsh, sir?' is not a question you are likely to be asked when you go shopping for samphire. Most of the samphire you will encounter today is marsh samphire (also known as glasswort), a succulent wild delicacy that grows on tidal marshes around Britain. Rock samphire is a rarer plant, with a pungent, sulphurous aroma and a tendency to grow in vertiginous places. Such was its value historically that pickers risked their lives to gather rock samphire, which earned mentions in *King Lear* and in Pepys' diaries. Its usage declined as it became more scarce, though rock samphire can still be found on south coasts in Britain. It also has an earlier season, being in its prime in spring rather than summer. However, unless you combine an interest in wild gastronomy with advanced abseiling skills, it seems unlikely that rock samphire will figure greatly in your seasonal diet.

Marsh samphire is more widely available. It can be obtained (for a price) from speciality food retailers, fishmongers or more widely on the Norfolk coast where it is best known as a delicacy. But the real fun of marsh samphire is the pick-your-own approach, which is considerably cheaper. If you happen to be in a coastal area between June and September, the samphire plants, which look like bright green miniature cacti, can be picked at low tide in tidal marshes. It's a muddy business, for it is said that the best samphire is covered by every tide. You will be well rewarded, though, for despite what hardcore rock samphire aficionados might say, marsh samphire is a fine salty delicacy with a succulent texture. It can be served like asparagus, briefly boiled and dipped in butter, or used to accompany a fish dish. Marsh samphire gets tougher as the season progresses and doesn't keep well (unless you pickle it) so it is perhaps best eaten as part of a summer holiday foraging session. Pick it sparingly, though. Marsh samphire is a winter food for certain birds, and can be a habitat for others.

September

Treats for the month

September	Seasonal Treats	Coming in	Going out
Vegetables	Mushrooms, wild Sweetcorn Tomatoes	Kale Swede	Beans, French Dandelion Peas Samphire Watercress
Fruit & Nuts	Blackberries Elderberries Plums and greengages Raspberries	Chestnuts Crabapples Damsons and bullaces Sloes	Blackcurrants and redcurrants Cobnuts Strawberries
Meat, Game & Poultry	Goose	Hare Mallard Partridge Rabbit	
Fish & Seafood		Eel Mussels Oysters, native	Sea trout

September

'Thus harvest ends its busy reign
And leaves the fields their peace again'

September marks a turning point in the year. It's the end of summer; the start of term; the beginning of autumn; and for farmers, it's the start of a new cycle of ploughing, planting and cultivation once the main harvest is in. It's also the time when the supply of fresh British seasonal food is at its peak for the year, with still-prime summer fruit and veg coinciding with the arrival of autumn and winter produce. More of autumn's tasty game starts to come in, although it's often good to wait until the creatures have had time for a bit more exercise before adding them to the menu. Michaelmas, at the end of September, was traditionally a time to eat geese that had grown fat on the gleanings from harvested fields.

September can be a tranquil, attractive month with settled weather and the countryside taking on autumn colours. It is certainly a good time to head out of town, for some of the main attractions of our wild harvest are now ready. Blackberries should be everywhere; it is a crime to miss out on them, as it is to forgo the more hard-won pleasures of elderberries, which are also ready now. The year's best jam- and jelly-making opportunities start here. And for the skilled, confident, or plain lucky, our increasingly popular wild mushroom season is just beginning. September is also when we can vote with our wallets for the great British plum, a superior product whose brief August–October season needs our support.

Blackberries, wild

Blackberries are the one connection that most of us have to the wild harvest in Britain. It is partly due to their accessibility: blackberries abound in hedgerows and at the edges of woodland, making them an easy wild snack even for those who don't like to stray too far from the car. The main reason, though, must surely be their quality. While not consistent in flavour – blackberries vary through their season and even from bush to bush – they are sweet enough to appeal to children yet subtle enough to keep the adults picking too.

The blackberry season runs from August until November and it is suggested that the early-ripening berries are the best. There is a celebrated taboo about not picking blackberries after 10 October, because during the night the Devil either spits, stamps or urinates (depending on which telling of the tale one reads) on every bush. The origin of this myth relates to Lucifer's having been cast out of heaven on Michaelmas Day (29 September), which corresponds with 10 October in the pre-1752 Julian calendar. One assumes that Old Nick saw the defiling of blackberries as an appropriate expression of his pique. The date probably has more to do with the fact that night frosts reduce the flavour of the fruit. Or maybe it relates to their position, often beside a road or path: by the end of the season, something is bound to have cocked a leg on them. So pick before the end of the season, and go for berries above waist height. Dorothy Hartley suggests a sequential picking, with the lowest, sweetest berries in each cluster (the first to ripen) to be eaten raw; the ones further up to be picked later for pies and puddings; and the highest to be picked latest in the season and mixed with apples on account of their high ratio of pips to pulp.

Blackberries do not keep well once picked, but they are a versatile late-summer fruit and well worth exploiting to the full. They make famous jelly, arguably the best there is, pair well with the season's apples for pies and jams, and are central to a good late summer pudding (*see p. 92*).

Blackberries are best enjoyed in season. Out-of-season imported varieties are ruinously expensive (especially when compared to the free wild harvest) and not a patch on the quality of the wild bramble. And who wants summer pudding in winter anyway?

Elderberries

Anyone who wants to get to know British seasonal produce better should become acquainted with elderberries. By September they are everywhere, hanging from their trees in beautiful bunches of tiny black berries, often with quite livid red stalks. Elderberries don't turn up in the shops: easy to crush, bulky to carry and quick to spoil, they don't fit easily into the modern food chain. So if you want elderberries, you have to go and get them yourself. It's not difficult: with a pair of scissors and a few carrier bags, a substantial haul can be quickly amassed. When the bunches of berries are hanging down, rather than pointing upwards, they are ready to pick. It's not as much fun as blackberrying, because elderberries contain a mildly poisonous alkaloid that renders them somewhat unpleasant when raw, so eating as you pick is not an option.

Once you've got them home, separating the berries from the stalks (traditionally done with a fork) is a time-consuming process. But elderberries are not about hurrying. The whole process of gathering and sorting the berries is a seasonal ritual at whose end lies the promise of pies, jams and jellies, and elderberry wine, rightly renowned as one of the finest country wines. Poet John Clare's brief description of gathering elderberries for wine (*see pp. 19–20*) is enough to make one want to get the demijohns ready for the next season.

The elder tree is the subject of much myth and folklore (*see also elderflower, p. 78*), which doubtless has much to do with the curative power of its fruit. *Wild Food* author Roger Phillips relates a story in which a nineteenth-century American sailor cited getting drunk on port as a remedy for rheumatic pains. After much investigation, it turned out that cheaper port was routinely adulterated with elderberry juice, known for its pain-relieving qualities.

Beyond wine, the traditional home for elderberries is in jelly; they pair well with apples or make good jelly on their own. And they also make excellent pies: a great seasonal pudding for days that are starting to get colder.

Elderberry pie
A simple and splendid pie.

250g/8oz plain flour
125g/4oz unsalted butter
750g–1kg (1½–2lb) elderberries
175–250g (6–8oz) sugar

First make the shortcrust pastry: rub together the flour and the butter until the consistency resembles breadcrumbs; then add a little water and form into a ball. Chill it for 30 minutes. Roll out just over half the dough until it is thinner than a pound coin, then line a greased pie dish with it. (This operation is made easier by using the rolling pin to pick up the pastry.)

Mix the elderberries with the sugar, then put them in the pie dish, slightly heaped in the middle. Roll out the rest of the dough to the same thickness as before, and, having moistened the rim of the pastry base, lay the 'lid' over the top of the pie. Trim the edge and press to seal it. Cut some slits to let the steam out, dust with more sugar and bake for 30 minutes at 220°C/425°F/gas 7.

Goose
Once, goose was one of the most seasonal of foods; now it seldom appears in the British diet at any time of year. The first dinner-table appearance of the domesticated goose was at Whitsuntide (late May/early June), when the six-week-old 'green goose' was traditionally eaten. It is suggested that gooseberries (*see p. xx*) may be so named because of the astringent fruit's affinity – and seasonal synchronism – with the young

bird. Geese that made it past this stage were eaten at Michaelmas (29th September). This was because Michaelmas was a 'quarter' day, on which debts and rents were paid. By this time, geese had been fattened on the post-harvest stubble, and made a fine meal and a gift for the landlord. Finally, geese were traditionally eaten at Christmas; they have been supplanted by turkey only relatively recently. In the seventeenth century, the birds were driven in the autumn from Norfolk to London in droves of up to a thousand birds, their feet having first been shod with a coating of tar and sand. Many small, mixed farms used to raise geese for sale at Christmas, a practice that has now been wiped out by food hygiene regulations.

Today, geese are raised by specialist producers, and the bird is widely available from September until Christmas. Geese are fortunate in that their difficult characters make intensive rearing impossible, so they are raised largely outdoors and in reasonably natural circumstances. *The Food We Eat* author Joanna Blythman observes that the limited consumer appeal of goose means there is not much incentive to engineer a bird that could put up with a crowded indoor life. So why is it that we eat comparatively little goose today? Partly it is to do with the bird's high ratio of fat to meat; it is messy to cook and difficult to carve. Despite that, its rich meat, infinitely superior to the turkey that has usurped its place at the Christmas dinner table, makes goose worth the effort.

The fat is another good reason for cooking a goose. In *Food in England*, Dorothy Hartley suggests at least twelve different applications for goose fat, from a sandwich filling to improving the quality of animal horns and hooves. The likeliest use for most people today, and surely the finest, is to make the very best roast potatoes known to man.

A goose can make a much more substantial feast if it is boned, then stuffed with a boned chicken that has itself been stuffed with a boned pheasant. It's hard work, but provides a lot of meat and a rich ceremonial dish. Hartley suggests an alternative of slipping a couple of rabbit legs inside the goose, which provides extra meat and ensures the rabbit is succulent. If you ever gaze hungrily on the geese in the park, your appetite is unlikely to be satisfied, however. Greylag, Canada and Pink-Footed geese can all be legally shot by wildfowlers in a September–January season they share with mallard (*see p. xx*), but despite the esteem in which their meat is held, such wild geese rarely turn up at specialist dealers.

Mushrooms, wild

Wild mushrooms are a vast subject to be covered in such a small space. There has been a surge of interest in them in recent years, before which time the British were among a minority of nations largely ignorant of the vast range of delicacies lurking in their fields and forests. Go to continental Europe in the autumn and the mushroom season is taken with great seriousness. Favourite spots are kept secret and there are ongoing clashes between commercial and casual pickers. And in France at least, most rural pharmacies will remove the Russian-roulette element from the mushroom-gathering process by identifying your freshly picked mushrooms and weeding out the killers. Back in Britain, wild mushrooms are available in speciality food shops and markets but do not come cheap, even in season.

Why autumn for this delicacy? The mushroom we eat is merely the tip of an iceberg: the 'fruiting body' of a greater organism consisting of microscopic subterranean threads that can spread far beyond the fruiting body itself. Many fungi have a symbiotic relationship with trees, helping them to take up water and nutrients. Studies in Sweden and Canada have suggested that the forming of mushrooms depends on a supply of 'photosynthate' – the sugars and carbohydrates produced by photosynthesis. In the autumn, as the trees shut down for the winter they divert this material below ground, where it becomes available to the fungi, enabling them to form mushrooms. Notable edible exceptions to this are morels (*see p. 58*) and St George's mushrooms, which appear in springtime. If you're picking wild mushrooms yourself, tag along with an expert or take great pains to ensure that you choose only those that belong to a safe species: the penalty for getting it wrong can be severe in the extreme.

A few meals with wild mushrooms will soon convince you that the effort or expense of tracking them down is justified. They may have little nutritional value, but their gastronomic worth is enormous. An omelette I was once served, made with newly laid eggs and just-picked wild mushrooms, went straight into my 'desert island dish' list. Ceps (boletus or porcini) are the number one target of many mushroom hunters. Simply sliced and fried, they provide a rich and earthy autumn starter. A culinary investment worth making at this time of the year is a mushroom brush: there's nothing worse than lovingly washing your hard-won ceps only to have them collapse into a mushy heap.

Plums and greengages

Is there anything worse than a bad plum? Probably not. But there are few things better than a good one. Sweet, juicy dessert plums are a great late-summer treat that follows on from the berry season; and cooking varieties produce richly flavoured desserts. Plums and greengages grow particularly well in our climate yet have a short season; the temptation to keep eating year-round supermarket supplies is strong, but rarely worth yielding to. However, even in the British season, from late July to October, we end up eating plums from afar. The imported fruit is often grown for size and ease of transport and picked before it is ripe, a treatment which improves nothing but the seller's profit margins.

The in-season British fruit, on the other hand, is justly famous for its superb quality and has been the subject of much horticultural development over the past few hundred years. The Brogdale Horticultural Trust nurtures 350 British varieties. So where are they all today? Like so much of our fruit, British plums have fallen victim to standardization and globalization, with much of what we eat now imported and only one or two varieties widely sold. Ironically, plums have also been hit by climate change. The trees have been flowering early with warmer spring weather, then succumbing to late frosts which can wipe out the fragile harvest. The picture is improving for the plum, however: the National Farmers' Union established August as Great British Plum Month, supported notably in 2003 by the Waitrose supermarket, which sold only British plums in the season.

Plums' short British season is spread over different varieties. It begins in late July and early August with dessert varieties (those that are good eaten raw) such as Early Laxton and Early Rivers, and Pershore and Czar for cooking; goes on through August with greengages (which are very fine dessert fruits) and the widespread dessert Victoria; then continues to September and shortly beyond with varieties such as Coe's Golden Drop for eating and Marjorie's Seedling for cooking. British dessert plums should colonize our fruitbowls during the season, while their cooking counterparts can make delightful puddings, sharpened in flavour if the skins are left on. A good way with them is to bake halved and stoned plums with a dusting of sugar and a bit of water: they collapse gracefully into soft and yielding fruit atop sweet, flavoursome syrup.

Raspberries

We are lucky to get two bites of the seasonal raspberry, with the fruits arriving in June or earlier, then getting properly into their stride in July. Then, just when it seems all over for what is famously a summer fruit, late varieties provide a second crop from September up until the first frosts. Raspberries are a delightful fruit, well suited to the British climate; and in particular to that of Scotland, which supplies up to 60 per cent of the raspberries eaten in Britain. The reason for this is that they mature slowly and do not need hot weather, but benefit from the long hours of summer daylight at northerly latitudes. Unlike the more stubborn blackberries, raspberries separate from their central 'receptacle' when picked so they are even more tender and easy to eat straight off the plant. Their sweetness varies through each variety's season, with the balance tending towards more sugar when the fruit is most mature and just about to fall off the plant on its own.

Fresh raspberries are such a summer treat that little can be done to them to improve the eating experience. If you are fortunate enough to be faced with a glut from your own or a pick-your-own crop, however, there are plenty of good things to do with raspberries. A Scottish seasonal home for them is the interior of a roast grouse. They are a core ingredient of summer pudding, the classic berry dish of an English summer; they make the freshest-tasting and most delicate jam there is, as well as superb ice creams for freezing. The berries themselves freeze reasonably well, as long as they are frozen flat on a tray first to create a collection of individual frozen berries and not a solid block of raspberry mush. Raspberry vinegar – in which the berries are steeped in white wine vinegar for a few days – has a dual role as a trendy cooking ingredient and a traditional remedy for a sore throat. Made into tea, the plant's leaves are therapeutic in the late stages of pregnancy and have been found to act beneficially on the pelvic muscles.

Where to find raspberries? They are widely available in their season but can be expensive, so growing or picking your own is an attractive option. Wild raspberries, famous for their flavour, are worth looking out for throughout Britain in woods, heathland and hilly areas. Wherever you find them, raspberries are one of the greatest delicacies of the British summer.

Sweetcorn

Sweetcorn is a type of maize, which, together with wheat and rice, is one of the three most important staple crops in the world. Despite this global prominence, it has had only a minor part to play in the British diet, mainly because we are at the northern edge of the area in which sweetcorn and maize can grow happily. That said, maize is an increasingly important crop in Britain, with over 100,000 hectares now grown in the south as animal fodder, mainly for the intensive dairy sector. Sweetcorn for human consumption accounts for a much smaller area. It is slow to develop and needs a good summer, with plenty of warm sunshine. The British crop matures just in time for the late-summer alfresco eating to which sweetcorn, with its slight exoticism, seems ideally suited.

Freshness is paramount with sweetcorn, as it is with peas and beans, for its sugars start converting to starches as soon as it is picked. Unless we have it growing in the garden, it seems unlikely that any of us will have the ultimate fresh sweetcorn experience: *Fork to Fork* author Monty Don suggests having a pan on the boil even before the cob is picked to minimize the time from plant to plate. Still, this is surely an argument for seeking out our own in-season produce, because a fresh sweetcorn cob that has been boiled until tender (5–10 minutes) then eaten with butter and pepper is a fine thing indeed.

There should be an element of 'buyer beware' with sweetcorn, however. Maize and sweetcorn growing is associated with a number of environmental depredations, from soil runoff (which silts up rivers) to the use of high levels of fertilizers, and the continuing use (until 2007 for sweetcorn) of Atrazine, a powerful herbicide that has been banned in many countries and is being withdrawn, albeit slowly, in Britain. So organic or grow-your-own is likely to be kinder to the countryside as well as your palate.

Tomatoes

Bursting with flavour that is a subtle balance between sweet and sharp, deliciously fragrant, and packed with vitamins and goodness, a good tomato is a wonderful thing. But how many fresh tomatoes answering to that description have you eaten recently? Not many, at most times of the year in Britain, would be my guess. Fresh tomatoes are, of course, available all year round. This constant abundance is achieved with a great deal of technology: indoor, controlled-atmosphere environments; artificial ripening; soil-free, hydroponic cultivation. The problem is that tomatoes don't want technology. They want to be outside. They taste best when they've had to work hard to reach a maturity whose final stages have been blessed with much fine, natural sunlight to give them the succulent sweetness tomato lovers crave. This of course means that in Britain outdoor tomatoes have a short season, with varieties available from around the end of July until October, depending on location. Tomatoes raised under glass – which make up the majority of cultivated tomatoes in Britain – will begin much earlier and last a little longer, say from March to November, but at the expense of eating quality.

The upshot of all this is that if you want a really good fresh British tomato, you have a short three-month time window, and you'll need to seek out small-scale growers, perhaps at farmers' markets. Or you could grow some yourself, because tomatoes are perfect for small-scale edible horticulture. All they need is a sunny spot, where they will grow happily in a pot or a grow-bag, given a bit of attention and a supply of tomato 'food' and water. The ritual of 'pinching out' unwanted shoots is all part of the fun, and the rich tomatoey smell this leaves on your hands is an appetizing foretaste of things to come.

If, by the end of the season, you have a glut, then what a perfect excuse to make vast quantities of pasta sauce for freezing (*see recipe*); or to experiment with bottling so you can avoid tasteless, woolly imports in the winter. And if your tomatoes haven't ripened by the end of the season, don't worry: green tomato chutney is a wonderful thing too.

A simple, fresh tomato sauce: The quality of this sauce depends entirely on the tomatoes: ripe, fresh, in-season ones are essential. Pour boiling water over 1.5kg/3lb of tomatoes in a large bowl. Finely chop two onions and four cloves of garlic and set to cook gently in lots of extra virgin olive oil. Drain off the water from the tomatoes, slip off their skins and quarter them, removing the seeds and cores. Chop the tomato flesh and add it to the onions and garlic. Bring it to the boil and simmer for 30 minutes. Season to taste. Use it with pasta or as a base for other sauces; it is best used immediately, or frozen.

Treats for the month

October	Seasonal Treats	Coming in	Going out
Vegetables	Cardoon Squash and pumpkins	Artichokes, Jerusalem Brussels sprouts Cabbage, red Cabbage, savoy Celeriac Celery Chicory Parsnips Salsify and scorzonera	Aubergines Beans, French Beans, runner Broccoli (calabrese) Courgettes Cucumber Rocket Tomatoes
Fruit & Nuts	Apples Chestnuts Crabapples Damsons and bullaces	Medlar Quince	Blackberries Blueberries Elderberries Loganberries Plums Raspberries Walnuts
Meat, Game & Poultry	Grouse Squirrel, grey	Pheasant Woodcock	Wood Pigeon
Fish & Seafood	Eels Oysters, native		Crab, brown

October

'Nature now spreads around in dreary hue
A pall to cover all that summer knew'

Take food out of the picture and October is not an attractive prospect. With clocks going back, it's getting darker and, with the first frosts, colder. In pre-Christian times, the end of October was the end of the year, a time of death and rebirth celebrated today as Hallowe'en. The last harvests meant everyone had to knuckle down for the hard months ahead. Animals were brought inside, some were slaughtered, and food was preserved for the winter. Temporarily fortunate pigs were turned out into the woods for 'pannaging': eating up the green acorns and beech mast that are poisonous to cattle and horses but make the pigs tastier. Down on the farm today, the hard winter work starts: fields are ploughed, winter wheat drilled, roots and potatoes harvested; and sheep are 'tupped' – the ram is put to the ewes.

From the perspective of the seasonal gourmet, though, October is a splendid time. Native apples are in peak condition. Succulent squash are ready to add flavour and body to seasonal dishes. Game abounds, with the pheasant and woodcock seasons opening in October and other birds plentiful. For those of us so inclined, it's not a bad time to eat a grey squirrel or two, because it's also a good month for the nuts they eat. Wild mushrooms are well in season as they continue the unsung but ecologically crucial task of transforming the nutrients that plants have absorbed back into elements that can be reused. October provides a fine seasonal banquet to fight the gathering gloom.

Apples

The British climate is well suited to growing apples. We have a rich heritage of dishes and drinks based around this fantastic fruit. Our National Fruit Collection at Brogdale in Kent lists 2,300 different varieties. As *The Book of Apples* reminds us, Britain can 'provide a greater diversity of varieties with the finest flavours in the world'. Yet, according to a Friends of the Earth survey conducted at the height of the British apple season, supermarkets, greengrocers and market stalls sell an average of three varieties. What's more, having grubbed up 60 per cent of our apple orchards since the 1970s, we now import the majority of our apples from overseas (France is our main supplier), with some travelling 20,000km before they reach our fruit bowls. To say this is madness, on both an ecological and a gastronomic level, is to understate enormously. We should be world leaders in apples. With judicious use of varieties and good storage, we can eat our own produce almost all year round, with perhaps a brief gap in July.

It's also worth seeking out our own apples from a nutritional point of view. Native varieties such as Discovery, Cox's Orange Pippin and Egremont Russet have anything from two to five times the vitamin C content of the bland Golden Delicious, Granny Smith and Red Dessert apples that flood our markets.

October, however, is the time to celebrate British apples. It is the moment when the British season is at its peak, with a mouth-watering array of varieties in prime condition. In this month, more than at any other time of the year, it should be our duty as consumers to seek out the best of our local apples from farmers' markets and good greengrocers. An organization called Common Ground has initiated 'Apple Day' in late October and claims some 600 events around the country: even supermarkets are starting to stock local varieties at this time. Perhaps the tide of interest in one of our finest home-grown fruits is turning.

A sample of British apples' seasonality

VARIETY	J	F	M	A	M	J	J	A	S	O	N	D
Discovery								○	●			
Worcester Pearmain									○	●		
Cox's Orange Pippin	●	●	●	●					○	○	●	●
Egremont Russet									○	○	●	●
Blenheim Orange	●								○	○	●	●
Nonpareil	●	●	●							○	●	●
Spartan	●	●	●							○	●	●
Bramley's Seedling	●	●	●	●	●	●				○	●	●

○ Picked Fresh   ● From Store (amateur storage)   ● From Store (commercial storage)

Source: *The Book of Apples*, Joan Morgan and Alison Richards

Cardoon

Cardoon! Not a Shakespearean insult, but a close relative of the globe artichoke (*see p. 90*). And not one that we see a great deal of in the shops or markets today. Cardoons have been a delicacy since Greek and Roman times, and have had a luxury reputation, alluded to by *British Housewife* author Martha Bradley when she wrote in the eighteenth century of cardoons being 'very agreeable at elegant tables'. This may stem from its close similarity to the globe artichoke, which was favoured by the aristocracy perhaps because of its one-time reputation as an aphrodisiac. Or it could be to do with the hassle of cardoon cultivation, which is probably a reason for its absence from our lives today.

It is the fleshy, celery-like stems of the cardoon that are eaten, rather than the unformed flower heads. However, they can't just be picked: the stems are blanched in the early autumn by surrounding the plant with a shield of cardboard or similar material to make them tender enough for eating. Even then, only the innermost stems are used. Together with the fact that cardoons take up a lot of garden space and can spread like a vigorous weed, all of this ritual does not make them a particularly economical crop to grow for food on a commercial scale. Now that the frisky aristocrats who might once have kept up a demand for cardoons have clearly moved on to other pleasures, they are a rarity today. Still, if you like your garden to look specta-cular, they provide tall plants (up to 2 metres) with colourful flowers, as well as an unusual gourmet delicacy for the late autumn. The stalks can be eaten raw, or boiled, or braised; perhaps they would add some extra luxury to pheasant braised with celery (*see p. 149*).

Chestnuts

A street vendor of chestnuts huddled over a cosy brazier in late autumn: what a quintessentially British sight. Or is it? Most chestnut cultivation happens in continental Europe, so it seems unlikely that your tasty bag of street chestnuts would be a local crop. The sweet chestnut tree, whose nuts hit the ground in mid-autumn, is, however, widespread in Britain and occurs as far north as central Scotland. So, for intrepid foragers, a real seasonal treat awaits. Sweet chestnut trees should not be confused with horse chestnuts, whose nuts have a traditional role as conkers but taste appalling. One way to tell them apart is by the leaves: those of the sweet chestnut are shaped like a spearhead, while the horse chestnut's leaves are almost pear-shaped.

Despite the profusion of sweet chestnut trees, and the nut's excellent gourmet value, chestnuts have not been widely esteemed for food in Britain. Elsewhere, particularly in southern Europe, they are eaten more widely and in more diverse ways; the starchy nut can be turned into bread, cakes, porridge and polenta. In Corsica, where the trees are common, they were a staple food and the major source of flour until the twentieth century. Still, chestnut processing is hard work and few of us are likely to go the distance needed to achieve chestnut flour from an October handful.

Throwing chestnuts in the embers of a fire is a traditional, obvious and delightfully seasonal thing to do on a cold autumn evening. Pricking them first to prevent explosion is essential, although *Food for Free* author Richard Mabey notes that the detonation of a single nut left unpricked will announce the readiness of the rest. Sweet chestnuts need little accompaniment; however, a mouthful of lukewarm milk after each nut is a bizarrely good pairing. Cooked chestnuts go extremely well with Brussels sprouts, thanks to a relationship in their flavour but a contrast in texture.

Crabapples

The wild ancestor to our domesticated apples, crabapples are unlikely to make much of an appearance in the shops. Like quinces, they are bitter and astringent if eaten raw. To make matters worse, they are small and therefore troublesome to harvest in great numbers. Crabapples do, however, have a lot going for them. Their spring blossom is a magnificent sight and smells wonderful, so planting them in the garden, if you have room, gives you two reasons for celebration each year. There are also crabapple trees to be found in the wild, where their small, table-tennis-ball-sized fruits vary from yellow to orange when ripe, depending on the species. The reason for bothering with crabapples? Jelly. Their astringency and high levels of pectin mean that they make an excellent, flavoursome jelly that pairs well with the season's game, or with fatty meats like shoulder of lamb. Making the jelly is an easy and enjoyable ritual.

Crabapple jelly: Put the washed fruit into a big pan, cover with water then simmer until soft, crushing the fruit into a pulp. Strain the mixture overnight through a jelly bag or muslin cloth (a tea towel will do): you can rig this up by tying the four corners of the cloth to the legs of an upturned chair. Time is important here, because pushing the pulp through to speed up the process may give you a cloudy jelly which is still tasty, but not as pretty. When the juice has all dripped through, dissolve sugar into it at a ratio of 1lb sugar to 1 pint juice (roughly 450g to 500ml), and boil rapidly until set. This should take 10–15 minutes. You can test for the 'setting point' by spooning some jelly on to a plate and cooling it a little; if it wrinkles when pushed with a finger, it's ready. Take it off the heat, then pot it in warmed jars.

Damsons and bullaces

As the summer turns to autumn, in-season members of the plum family get smaller and more hardy, culminating in the sloe (*see p. 140*), which can be picked up until November. In between the sweet summer plum and the sharply astringent sloe can be found damsons and bullaces. As long ago as the eighteenth century, these had already been eclipsed, as Martha Bradley drily observed in *The British Housewife*: 'There are two very mean ones which are yet very excellent, these are the Damson and the Bullace; the first has been put out of repute by many new fashioned kinds, the French names of which, are their greatest recommendation; and the other being esteemed a wild plumb is little regarded.'

Since Bradley wrote, the damson has had varied fortunes. It was grown particularly in the Midlands and North-west of England and its juices were valuable for dyeing wool. There is little commercial growing today, so damsons won't appear in many shops (and the bullace is strictly a wilderness treat). But Cumbrian damsons at least are enjoying a resurgence of interest, with the Westmoreland Damson Association setting out to restore the area's orchards. The fruit is celebrated there when the trees blossom in April (*see p. 24*), and is widely sold from mid-September to early October.

Damsons are better cooked than raw, their sharpness making them a fine ingredient for jams, jellies, ice cream, wine and damson gin. An old-fashioned recipe has them turned into 'damson cheese', a solid jam whose flavour is enhanced by adding the kernels from the fruit's stones.

Eels

Eels' bizarre life cycle – in which they breed in the Sargasso Sea, leaving their young to drift to Europe on the Gulf Stream as larvae – gives eel-fanciers two chances of a prime seasonal meal. In March the tiny elvers begin heading into British rivers, and offer a rare and expensive delicacy (*see p. 50*). Elvers mature into 'yellow eels', which spend anything from two to twenty years in fresh water before something – perhaps temperature changes and tides – tells them to head back west to spawn. Eels have never been observed breeding, nor been seen in the ocean returning to the Sargasso Sea. Truly mysterious creatures. When, in the autumn, eels are ready to head back to sea, they change colour and become 'silver eels'; sleek, fat, ready for their epic return journey and also in prime eating condition. This is when amateur fishermen and professional eel-smokers like to get hold of them.

While catching, killing and preparing eels – they need to be fresh – is a job for the committed and unsqueamish, eating them should really be for everyone. It's not easy to get hold of British silver eels, though: ironically, much of our catch goes to Europe while we import farmed eels. However, succulent smoked eel can be obtained direct from smokeries, particularly in Scotland where the river Tweed provides a copious supply. And in London, where eels are now caught in the Thames again, at least some of the catch goes to the remaining pie-and-mash shops in the city.

Smoked and fresh eel is available all year round, but mid-autumn is when British eels are at their best. As with many fish species, though, eel populations are under serious pressure. European eels cannot reproduce in captivity, so the (big) global business of eel aquaculture is dependent on wild elvers: a state of affairs that does not seem at all sustainable. A Europe-wide stock recovery plan is being put in place to halt the decline in numbers. So seasonal gourmets should view British silver eels as a very occasional treat, and perhaps question the value of buying the farmed creatures.

Grouse

Grouse are about as seasonal as it gets. They are not the only game bird that can be shot on 12 August, the beginning of the shooting season: the less well-known ptarmigan and snipe are also in the firing line that day. It is their larger size and their eating quality, however, that have led to the grouse's fame as the first (and some would say finest) game bird of the season.

There may be nothing particularly 'natural' about grouse shooting, but the whole subject is more complex than it might seem. Shooting grouse is an expensive business (which is why the end result is such a costly roast dinner) and is thus traditionally the preserve of the corporately financed, or of the aristocracy, who championed the sport in the mid-nineteenth century. This is doubtless part of the reason why the sport is now a target of the anti-hunt lobby. Another might be that it seems a bit of a turkey shoot. Grouse like to sit hidden by heather for much of the time, so have to be flushed out by beaters from their hiding places, whence they fly towards the camouflaged guns in a straight line. They're fast, though, so it's not quite so easy.

The other 'unnatural' element of grouse shooting – and a further reason for its expense – is that the heather moorland on which grouse thrive needs to be actively managed. This involves, among other things, controlled burning of the heather to ensure a mosaic of plants at different growth stages to provide both food and cover for the birds. So some argue that, paradoxically, without grouse shooting we would not have beautiful heather moorlands full of different bird species. And they have a point. In *The Killing of the Countryside*, author Graham Harvey points out that in Shropshire similar careful management of common moorland for grazing by generations of commoners ensured a biodiversity that more intensive sheep rearing is now eradicating. But the alleged poisoning of birds of prey by moorland gamekeepers is drawing the ire of the conservation lobby and providing ammunition for the sport's opponents. This may, ironically, one day spell the end of a land management practice that itself conserves a wide range of bird species, not just grouse.

So grouse are complicated, and costly, although the price drops as the season progresses. But they are still worth it as a restaurant treat (if you're feeling flush), or as the centrepiece of a smart autumn dinner, for which they need to be larded with bacon fat, optionally stuffed with butter and seasonal raspberries, roasted quickly and at great heat, and served with game chips and perhaps a root vegetable purée. Maybe the cost of grouse is a price worth paying for the moorland biodiversity their continued existence can help ensure.

Oysters, native

Marked by festivals around the south coast in both September and October, the beginning of the oyster season is a serious cause for seasonal celebration. The old saw about not eating oysters in a month not containing the letter 'r' has to do with the contention that they spawn in the warmer summer waters in some areas and can be undesirably milky, fat and soft. The tastier, 'native' oysters have been exploited for centuries in a trade that centres around the Thames estuary and the famous oyster towns of Colchester and Whitstable. Up until the late nineteenth century, oysters were highly abundant and were used to thicken and bulk out stews as well as being eaten on their own. Eight gallons of oysters could be had for a mere fourpence in the eighteenth century. However, a combination of economics, disease and bad weather decimated the stocks and turned oysters into the rather costlier delicacy they have become today.

Now, natives are farmed alongside Pacific oysters, which are less valued than natives (but still well worth the bother) and available all year round. If you plan on eating oysters at home, invest in an oyster knife. The few pounds it will cost is a small price to pay to avoid the injuries that can result from tackling an oyster with unsuitable kit. I still wince at the memory of a failed Swiss-army-knife attempt. Raw, with the usual zingy accompaniments of lemon juice or Tabasco, oysters make one of the most invigorating amuse-gueules available; gently grilled, with buttery sauces, they are a sensual treat.

Squash and pumpkins

Like all members of the *cucurbit* family, pumpkins are an American import. They do not seem to have much of a history of inclusion in the British gastronomic canon, our main association with them being as scary containers for a Hallowe'en candle. In the US, pumpkins are also associated with thanksgiving celebrations, when they are eaten as a dessert in pumpkin pie. The smaller, tastier examples are, however, now to be seen more and more in farmers' markets and organic box schemes, where they have become a welcome seasonal treat. Pumpkins are also extremely easy and entertaining to grow, as long as you have the space to contain their wild spreading season, when the vine-like tendrils grow at an astonishing pace. Not ideal for the tiny urban garden.

Concentrating most of their goodness into their seeds (which are worth toasting), pumpkins do not abound in nutritional value. But they keep for ages and contribute great flavour and body to seasonal dishes, particularly when roasted. The seasonally orientated *River Café Cook Book Green* has a superb recipe in which pumpkin flavours a pasta filling. If you think life is too short to do the home pasta-making this recipe demands, then chopped, roasted pumpkin served simply with butter and pepper is very good indeed. If, however, you are feeling adventurous (and you have a pasta machine, which makes things a great deal easier), the effort is well rewarded. A simplified version of the recipe appears overleaf.

Pansoti with pumpkin

This is a lot of work, but it beats turning a pumpkin into a scary Hallowe'en face.

1 orange-fleshed eating pumpkin
salt and freshly ground pepper
a handful each grated Parmesan
and ricotta
3 eggs, beaten
2 cloves garlic, finely chopped

a small handful breadcrumbs
500g/1lb home-made pasta, rolled
into thin sheets the width of the
pasta machine
butter and Parmesan to serve

First make the filling: cut the pumpkin into slices (maybe keeping the seeds for roasting), season it, then roast it at 200°C/400°F/gas 6 until soft. Push it through a mouli, then mix it with the Parmesan and ricotta cheeses, the eggs, chopped garlic and breadcrumbs until you have a tasty orange purée.

Put tablespoonfuls of the filling at 10cm intervals down the middle of each sheet of pasta, then fold the pasta lengthways and press round the filling to create little mounds. Cut these out in semicircles, then leave on a floured tray to dry for a while. (This is, incidentally, easier than making ravioli, which need a sandwich of two pasta sheets.) Cook the pansoti in batches, for 5 minutes in boiling salted water, removing them with a slotted spoon. Serve immediately with melted butter and more freshly grated Parmesan.
Serves six as a starter.

Squirrel, grey

To many urban dwellers, they are cute, semi-tame reminders that somewhere the world is still full of delightful furry wildlife. To some country people, particularly gamekeepers, they are a pest. To their protected red relatives, they are a vicious imposter who has pushed them to the fringes of Britain and towards possible extinction. To Americans (from whose country they came here around 130 years ago), they are classified as game and are a popular huntsman's quarry and meal. Whatever your view of grey squirrels, the fact is that they are overabundant (with a population estimated at 2.5 million), officially classified as vermin, and from October into the winter, when they start tucking into the season's diet of nuts, extremely good to eat. This means that if you are dedicated to both ecology and gastronomy, the squirrel should be in your sights.

You will probably have to do the job yourself, because although at least one English butcher and one smart London restaurant are known to provide it, squirrel is not widely stocked. An air rifle will do the trick, or a squirrel trap. But beware the animal rights-minded: their emotional attachment to furry vermin (which often coincides with an indifference to the infinitely grimmer fates of intensively reared farm animals) is a factor that the amateur squirrel hunter should consider. Eat the haunches only, grilled or stewed, depending on age.

November

Treats for the month

November	Seasonal Treats	Coming in	Going out
Vegetables	Brussels sprouts Cauliflower		Mushrooms, wild Sorrel
Fruit & Nuts	Medlars Pears Quince Sloes		
Meat, Game & Poultry	Mallard Partridge, grey		Lamb, new season
Fish & Seafood	Mussels		Lobster Mackerel

November

'When frost locks up the streams in chill delay
And mellows on the hedge the purple sloes'

Our forebears' livestock must have looked upon November with some anxiety. This was traditionally the time when, fat with the season's produce but potentially a liability for the lean winter months, all but an essential few were slaughtered. The introduction of winter fodder crops put an end to this annual carnage by enabling both man and his animals to thrive through the winter. Sadly, November is no longer a feast of black pudding and faggots: but there's plenty on offer for the modern seasonal gourmet.

Changes in the weather are now dictating what is available: any vegetables that can't stand frost will have to be harvested or stored. But the cold weather also brings gains: some fruit and veg, such as sloes, parsnips and kale, are positively improved by frost. Now is the time to start seeking them out. Although the countryside is beginning to look barren at this time of year, it still has fruit to offer – not just sloes and late pears, but also quinces and medlar, which offer rare treats of perfumed desserts and excellent preserves. The game season is now in full swing, and the seasonal larder offers fine combinations of rich meats, root vegetables and sharp jellies. Adding to this comforting store are Brussels sprouts, a seasonal treat which deserves more than its apologetic annual appearance at the Christmas dinner table. For an alternative treat try mussels, which are in peak condition at this time of year and, with chips, a fine complement to a warming autumnal beer.

Brussels sprouts

The Brussels sprout needs our support. It is the only vegetable with an almost universally well-known seasonal place at the British table, as part of the Christmas feast. Yet apart from its annual appearance alongside the turkey, the sprout is often shunned, despite being delicious, nutritious and in season through the winter months (from around November to March) when we most need tasty and nourishing food. Not only that, it offers two separate delicacies: the sprout itself and the sprout tops, the leaves at the very top of the tall sprout plant that are, in essence, an unformed apex sprout. Traditionally eaten later, when all the other sprouts have been picked off the plant, sprout tops are tender, tasty and make an excellent side dish just steamed and served with perhaps a little butter.

As with many of its brassica brethren, it is likely that the bad reputation of Brussels sprouts comes from memories of smelly, soggy childhood servings, which may – at least in part – have been due to the practice of scoring a cross on the sprout's base, which is really only necessary for the largest ones. Sprouts should still have a bit of 'bite' when they are done, to ensure the optimum texture and flavour. Brief cooking also retains their considerable nutritional value.

Happily, there are moves afoot to rehabilitate the sprout. A festival held in its honour in November (*see p. 25*) celebrates everything to do with the vegetable; and at farmers' markets, sprouts are starting to be sold on their rather attractive stalk, which makes the purchase a bit more of an event and helps the sprouts to keep a little longer. And there are a surprising number of tasty ways to prepare sprouts, beyond the obvious brief boiling or steaming: finely chopped, they can be stir-fried with, of all things, sun-dried tomatoes to create a zesty little dish. Their flavour works well alongside braised red cabbage or chestnuts (or both); in the *Four Seasons Cookery Book*, Margaret Costa suggests using a blender to make a bright purée out of lightly cooked sprouts and cream. It's high time Brussels sprouts, versatile, tasty and extremely good for us, came in from the cold.

Cauliflower

The cauliflower's many varieties have almost deprived it of seasonal status. The Henry Doubleday Research Association's *Encyclopaedia of Organic Gardening* lists no fewer than six seasonally nuanced types: spring, early summer, late summer, early autumn, autumn and winter. So there is no time of the year when we need be without British, in-season cauliflower (although location is important: winter-maturing cauliflower needs a mild climate like the South-west's). When we eat cauliflower is, therefore, a matter of choice rather than seasonal diktat.

But do we want to eat it? Along with most members of the brassica family – Brussels sprouts, cabbage, broccoli – the consumption of cauliflower has a hair-shirt hinterland of sulphurous overboiling and childhood revulsion. This isn't really fair, though; it harks back to an age of austerity and to a grimly practical British attitude to food which has changed much for the better. If cooked lightly, cauliflower is both tasty and nutritious. Like broccoli, its heads are made up of unopened flower buds that have stopped growing, and the nutrients that would have been used to power the flowers are stored in the stalks. The exhortations of our elders and betters to finish up our cauliflower were well placed, for it is rich in vitamins and goodness.

How and when to eat it is a highly subjective area. The florets can be eaten raw, in which state they will be most highly nutritious; yet even the most calorific mayonnaise in the world doesn't seem to make this a particularly attractive prospect, however beneficial it might be. Cauliflower's natural role is as a comfort food. Cauliflower cheese can be dreadful, but it can also be superb. You could bake it for ages with a sauce made of bland, rubber cheese; or you could boil the separate florets quickly, then pour over a rich sauce made with the finest Cheddar and maybe boosted with a little Dijon mustard. Could this be the ultimate hangover cure, returning warmth and goodness to a battered system? And as to season, cauliflower's comforting qualities seem suited to the autumn, when it is widely available and ready to insulate us from winter's coming chill.

Mallard

If you think that most of the duck sold today has had a happy life dabbling in ponds before its final journey to the shops, think again. The duck that is most widely available throughout the year is raised indoors, in the kind of intensive systems more commonly associated with chicken. For duck to be relatively cheap, and in abundance all year, this is the price to be paid today: cottage-based duck rearing has long since fallen victim to hygiene regulations and economies of scale.

Do we really want duck all year round, though? It seems particularly unnatural for such water-loving creatures to spend their short lives crowded into a shed. If you would prefer your duck to have had at least a swim before it ends up on your plate, you'll need to look to wild duck; and thus to the seasons.

Mallard – the familiar, rather beautiful duck of parks and ponds – is top of a list of nine duck species that can be legally shot in Britain. Its season runs from 1 September to the end of January, or to 20 February below the high-water mark. Mallard cannot be guaranteed to be truly wild, because some are reared before release. As with pheasant (*see p. 149*), this means it is worth waiting until well into the season before seeking out mallard: by then they will have spent some time on a healthy, muscle-building regime of wild food and exercise. So November and December are acknowledged to be the best times to look for mallard at good butchers and on the menus of good restaurants. They are a popular game quarry, so in plentiful supply.

The practice of wildfowling, as with much hunting, excites great passion in its followers. It seems a shame (although it is probably a very good thing for the species' survival) that the 'punt gun' is now such a rarity in Britain. There is something darkly comic – albeit tremendously unsporting – about a great floating cannon, seemingly better suited to naval warfare, being trained on a flock of unsuspecting wildfowl. These days, mallard are usually shot in a fairer and more conventional way.

They are easy to cook: a hot thirty-minute roasting produces a succulent pink, gamey feast. Orange, the classic accompaniment to roast duck, is available all year round, but there is a short overlap between the mallard and Seville orange seasons in January that makes possible the best pairing. Apple is recommended with duck, as is braised red cabbage: both of these are also good seasonal matches.

Salmi of wild duck

Adapted from Margaret Costa's Four Seasons Cookery Book, *this makes the most of mallard's rich flavour.*

2 mallard	1 tablespoon plain flour
butter for basting the birds	150ml/^{1}/4 pint port
1 onion (or 3 shallots), chopped	1 tablespoon redcurrant jelly
1 carrot, chopped	the juice of 1 orange and 1 lemon
1 stick of celery, chopped	the finely shredded rind of ^{1}/2 orange,
2 bay leaves	blanched
115g/4oz mushrooms	salt and freshly ground pepper
25g/1oz butter	cayenne pepper

Rub the duck breasts with butter and put some more inside the birds. Roast at 220°C/425°F/gas 7 for 20 minutes, basting several times. Remove the wishbones, then slice off the meat from the breasts and legs.

Chop and pound the carcasses, and put them in a saucepan with the giblets and necks (if you have them), the chopped vegetables, bay leaves and mushrooms. Cover with water, bring to the boil and simmer for an hour or so. Strain off the stock and, if necessary, boil hard to reduce so you have 425ml/^{3}/4 pint.

Melt 25g/1oz butter, blend in the flour and cook until it is brown; then gradually add the stock, stirring over a gentle heat until you have a smooth, creamy sauce. Add the port, redcurrant jelly, orange and lemon juice; season to taste with salt, pepper and cayenne. Add the blanched orange rind. Gently reheat the pieces of duck in the sauce. Serve with mashed potatoes and seasonal vegetables.
Serves six.

Medlars

Like a rook or an elver, a medlar is a delicacy likely to be savoured only by the most determined of seasonal gourmets. Popular in Victorian times, its unusual flavour and difficult habits have condemned it to a position of relative obscurity today. The medlar is related to the apple and the quince, and is a hardy fruit that flowers attractively in May and ripens in late October and November. 'Ripening' is not a strictly appropriate term, for medlars originate in warmer climates and in Britain they never ripen sufficiently to be eaten off the tree. So in November the fruit, which resembles a large, russet-coloured rose hip, is still hard and inedible. In this state it can, like a British quince, be made into an excellent jelly.

To eat a raw medlar, you must first let it rot for a few weeks, a process called 'bletting', which is defined as 'an internal decay without external sign'. In the medlar's case, this decay takes the form of a fermentation that is partially responsible for its peculiar flavour, variously described as 'off', 'astringent', 'truffle-like' and 'aromatic'. Given that the medlar is also visually somewhat unappealing, it is not surprising that the more timid palates of the twentieth century rejected it. The Victorian way with a bletted medlar was to combine the scraped-out pulp with sugar and cream, and wash it down with a glass of port. Sounds like an autumn tradition worthy of revival. Medlars are grown by gardeners and can be found occasionally in hedgerows in the south and east of England.

Mussels

Mussels are one of the few seafoods whose purchase need not embroil the conscientious buyer in a complex ethical debate. They are in plentiful supply and their artificial cultivation increasingly happens in a way that creates a fine specimen and has a minimal impact on the environment. So in autumn and winter, when mussels are at their fattest and best, the seasonal gourmet should be out looking for them: they are easy to cook, tasty and succulent, and relatively inexpensive.

Some may fear mussels for their 'Russian roulette' reputation. This stems from the fact that they are filter feeders, pumping up to ten gallons of water a day in a bid to extract the plankton on which they feast. Even more so than with other edible bivalves (two-sided shellfish), the quality of mussels depends very much on the water in which they grow. For this reason, gathering them in the wild (where they remain plentiful) is risky where there is any chance of contamination from sewage or from 'red tide' algal blooms.

Today, one can eat mussels with confidence as long as their provenance is known. Many mussels are now grown on long ropes attached to rafts, in the relatively clean waters of Scotland and Ireland: these are the ones to seek out, not only for their cleanliness but also for the fact that, unlike dredged mussels, their shells are undamaged by the harvesting process.

The variety that lives in Britain, the blue or common mussel, is small; bigger varieties, such as the Pacific green-lipped mussel, can be had in this country, but it seems a shame to make a poor bivalve travel all that distance. Small, in this case, is beautiful, and perfect for the Belgian classic *moules frites* (mussels and chips), a dish ideally suited for adoption by the British. Never mind all the fancy things one might attempt with mussels – simmering them in a little white wine until they open, then serving them with chips and a sauce made of the cooking juices and some butter seems like the obvious thing to do. Particularly when it is also customary to wash them down with high-quality artisanal beer. Never underestimate the Belgians: they have the highest density of Michelin-starred restaurants in Europe. An eating tip – use the shell of the first mussel like a pair of tongs to pick out the rest.

Mussels should always be alive and closed when bought. If any open ones fail to close when tapped, they are dead and should be discarded.

Partridge, grey

Small, attractive, grey, tasty, hangs about in pear trees. The last part is unlikely; the rest is an accurate description of the grey partridge, a long-time inhabitant of Britain and a popular game bird. These days, however, partridges have been hanging about in fewer and fewer places. Their lifestyle makes traditional agricultural land the perfect habitat for them, with hedges for nesting and shelter, and abundant food in the form of insects and seeds. Young partridges need a high-protein diet, preferably of insects, for their first three weeks of life. Sadly, the insects and their habitats have been banished by the widespread use of pesticides and herbicides in farming. Hedgerows have disappeared as fields have become ever bigger. So the modern partridge often has nothing to eat and nowhere to hide, and populations have crashed by 85 per cent in the last thirty years. The grey partridge is now a 'biodiversity action plan' species, and measures are being taken to encourage farmers to manage set-aside land for wildlife and to create margins between crops that the birds can use. As a result, the partridge is staging a slow recovery in its heartlands of the east of England and Scotland.

Partridges, which made up much of the bag of game birds shot in the early 1900s, are also routinely reared for shooting. Not on the same scale as pheasant (*see p. 149*), which is now bred and released in vast numbers, but to the extent that the partridge you encounter commercially is unlikely to be truly wild. So, as with pheasant, it is worth waiting until the season progresses, say until October or November, before putting a partridge in your pot.

Younger birds can simply be roasted; older ones braised or stewed with seasonal partners such as savoy cabbage, root vegetables or apples. The grey partridge's red-legged cousin also lives in Britain, but is more popular in France where its meat is esteemed; however, its unsporting reluctance to fly makes it a less popular game target over here.

Pears

Pears are another fruit that should incite us to rise up and rebel against our crazy food chain. Although they are less hardy than apples (*see p. 122*), pears grow well in Britain and 550 different varieties – earlies, lates, dessert pears, cooking pears, pears for making perry – are listed by the National Fruit Collection. Gloucestershire alone has a mighty range, rejoicing in names like Bloody Bastard and Clipper Dick. Yet over 90 per cent of the pears sold in the UK are of just three varieties; and super-markets import up to 75 per cent of their apples and pears. It's the same lunacy that brings us bland apples when we live in a country that can produce the finest in the world: an obsession with uniformity, cheapness, storage and transport, and uncomplicated cultivation.

If you are looking for interesting British pears in their season – which runs from as early as August through to the last of the stored pears as late as March – supermarkets may have some, but local growers and retailers, farmers' markets and your own trees are the best bets. Express your pear rebellion by buying locally, where at all possible. It's also worth seeking out organic produce, for pears are sometimes treated with post-harvest preservative chemicals.

The ripening of pears is a complex business. They are not left to ripen on the tree, but picked when still hard, whereafter they will ripen in your fruit bowl. Catching them at just the right moment is a matter of trial and error, for once past their brief period of perfect ripeness, pears can become 'sleepy' (mealy) and unpleasant. A crisper pear is a good accompaniment for a hard and nutty cheese; a delicate dessert can be had by stewing them gently with red wine and cinnamon, and they have a famous affinity with chocolate.

Quince

Related to the apple but much harder to find, quinces are well worth seeking out when their season begins around October. If you're lucky enough to be in an enclosed space next to a big yellow pile of quinces, you will enjoy the most delicate and intoxicating aroma. As this smell lasts for some time, it's worth keeping them for a week or so as a posh air freshener before getting down to the business of eating them.

Resist the temptation to chomp into a quince, because they are not good to eat raw. Buying quinces means more work, but it's well rewarded. Cored and grated, they add flavour and colour to apple pie. Stewed, baked or poached with sugar or honey they make a luxuriously refreshing dessert in their own right. Quinces make great marmalade, and a block of quince 'cheese', a sliceable preserve, is a fine accompaniment to real cheese at the end of a meal.

Quinces poached in muscat
This recipe adapted from Nigella Lawson's How to Eat *involves the extravagant use of fine dessert wine for cooking purposes, but the end result is so good that the expense is quickly forgotten.*

4 quinces	1 cinnamon stick
lemon juice	2 bay leaves
700ml/1½ pints muscat	3 cloves
500ml/1 pint water	3 cardamom pods
500g/1lb sugar	6 peppercorns

Peel, core and quarter the quinces, and drop them into a bowl of water with a squirt of lemon juice. (Keep the quince trimmings.)

Bring to the boil the muscat, water and sugar in a pan together with the cinnamon stick, bay leaves, cloves, cardamom pods and peppercorns.

Put the quince peel and cores in an ovenproof dish with the quartered quinces and the muscat syrup. Cover securely with a lid or with foil, and cook for 2^1/2 hours at 160°C/325°F/gas 3. Let it cool.

Remove the now brick-red quince quarters with a slotted spoon and place in a serving bowl; then strain the syrup into a pan and reduce it, tasting (mindful of its heat) until it's where you want it. Let it cool slightly and pour over the quinces. Serve with crème fraiche or yoghurt. Any syrup left over is superb with ice cream or for a furtive, decadent sip from the fridge.
Serves up to eight.

Sloes

Sloes have one association for most people: sloe gin. Dorothy Hartley implies that it was sloe gin that gained the celebrated nickname 'Mother's Ruin', on account of its having 'long been used by old-fashioned country wives in connubial emergencies'. One cannot help but speculate as to what form such delicately named episodes took. Meanwhile, though, sloes are an excellent seasonal treat, and not only for what they do to gin.

Fruiting from around September to November, the sloe is the small, astringent ancestor of modern cultivated plums, much as the crabapple (*see p. 124*) is a wild relative of contemporary apple varieties. Like crabapples, sloes are far too bitter to eat raw; and they are not sold commercially, so those wishing to enjoy sloes have work to do. The gathering, however, is part of the fun of autumn. Finding them is not difficult: the blackthorn tree on which sloes grow is a tough shrub that reaches one to four metres in height and is found throughout Britain in hedges, woods and scrubland. The ripe berries are a deep, dusty purple. Although sloes are around from September onwards, it is worth waiting until after the first frosts, particularly if you are making gin: frost makes the skins more permeable and tempers the astringency a little.

Sloe gin: Making sloe gin is simply a question of half filling empty wine bottles with the pricked berries, topping up with gin and half the berries' weight in sugar, and stoppering. Time (at least two months, preferably longer) and the occasional shake will finish the job and produce a livid red, powerfully warming drink. But gin is not the end of it for sloes. They also make excellent jelly, whose sharp flavour goes well with the season's game.

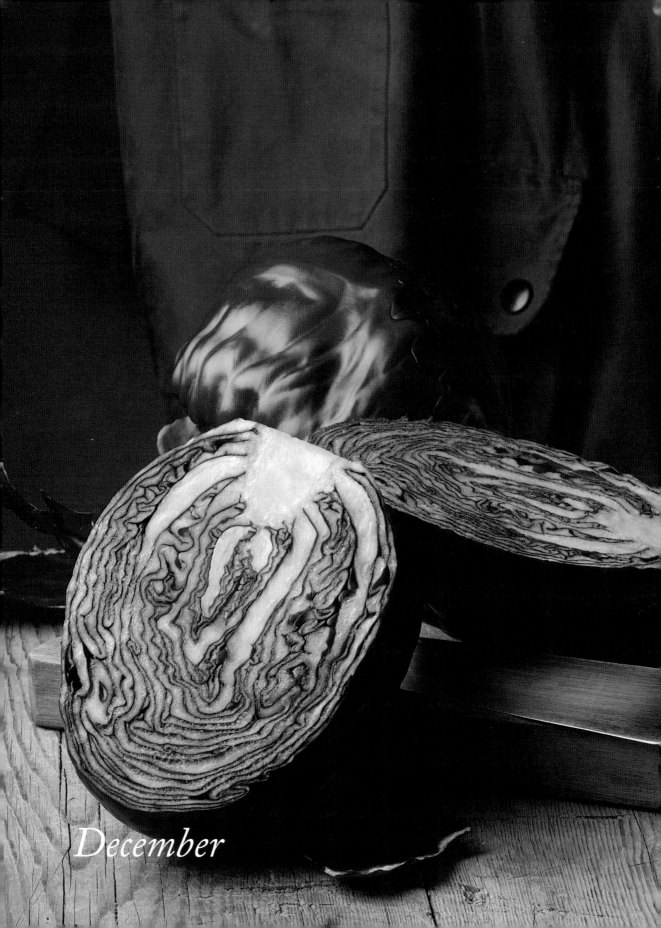

December

Treats for the month

December	Seasonal Treats	Coming in	Going out
Vegetables	Artichokes, Jerusalem Cabbage, red Celeriac Celery Parsnips		Cardoon
Fruit & Nuts			Chestnuts Quince
Meat, Game & Poultry	Pheasant Turkey Woodcock		Grouse Squirrel, grey
Fish & Seafood			

December

*'The yule cake dotted thick wi plumbs
Is on each supper table found'*

The only month of the year that retains a major seasonal gastronomic event in Britain, December is truly a time for the gourmet. Christmas has its roots in many different traditions, notably that of marking the turn of the year – the winter solstice on 21–22 December. At this time, many cultures celebrated the 'return' of the sun, as days started to get longer and the land came slowly back to life. Even for our hard-pressed ancestors, this pivotal point in the year was a time to take a break and celebrate. Although it's not the coldest month, the brief daylight hours and the bare countryside give December days a gloomy feel: it seems entirely appropriate to take solace in fine seasonal produce.

This is a time of year for perfect pairings of foods that are in their prime. Celery and Stilton cheese, for example, should taste better now than at any other time. Any remaining chestnuts will go well with braised red cabbage. And the enduring partnership of roast game and winter vegetables continues.

December is, of course, the time of year that turkeys fear: the very best ones are bred specifically for Christmas, making high-quality turkey the most seasonal of meat. Geese, too, should be getting uneasy in December, for they are enjoying renewed popularity as the central attraction of a festive meal. The seasonal gourmet has little to worry about at this time of year, though: rich, warm, comforting food abounds.

Artichokes, Jerusalem

A great winter treat, Jerusalem artichokes are nonetheless afflicted by some confusion and a little – perhaps justified – reluctance on the part of consumers. For a start, they have no ties to Jerusalem: their name is apparently a corruption of *girasole* (Italian for sunflower), given to them because some varieties produce sunflower-like blooms. Neither do they have any relation to the globe artichoke: their flavour was likened to globe artichokes on their early-seventeenth-century introduction from North America, hence the name.

Jerusalem artichokes are a small, knobbly tuber with, as Dorothy Hartley suggests, a 'very individual flavour', sweet and nutty. They are easy to grow, but only if you have enough space: Jerusalem artichoke stems can grow up to two metres tall and create a dense thicket in which not much else can thrive. Which is fine if you have a big garden and want a windbreak, a weed-free zone or (surprisingly) a pheasant magnet: a big stand of Jerusalem artichokes is very alluring to these tasty birds. What better way to get a complete seasonal meal lined up in one place?

As for eating, Jerusalem artichokes are surprisingly versatile. They can be boiled, fried, roasted, chipped, or eaten raw and added to salads. Jane Grigson and Margaret Costa both suggest a pairing with scallops. Their flavour, however, combined with a tendency to soften quickly when boiled, makes soups and purées an ideal outcome for a Jerusalem artichoke. So why the reluctance on behalf of potential consumers? Flatulence. Jerusalem artichokes contain a mostly indigestible substance called inulin which can lead to a degree of physical (and social) discomfort. This is no reason to avoid the tubers, for they really are excellent; but perhaps they are better served at lunch, so that relief from their after-effects may be sought in the open air of a post-prandial stroll.

Jerusalem artichoke soup

This is a particularly easy soup to make, with an excellent flavour. To prevent the artichokes discolouring while you are peeling and chopping them, drop them into a bowl of water into which you've briefly squeezed a lemon. Adding a dollop of cream before serving relieves the soup's rather dowdy colour.

1 medium onion, chopped	1 litre/2 pints good chicken stock
a splash of olive oil	salt and freshly ground pepper
1kg/2lb Jerusalem artichokes, peeled and chopped	double cream to serve

Cook the onion gently in the oil until soft. Add the chopped artichokes and the stock, bring to the boil and simmer until the artichokes are cooked and soft.

Liquidize or sieve, adding more stock if the soup is too thick. Season to taste. Add a dollop of cream to each portion.
Serves six.

Cabbage, red

Red cabbage may well be just another tough, 'tight-headed' cabbage; a more attractive version of the uninspiring white varieties that are a feature of the winter months. There's something about it, though, that elevates red cabbage to seasonal treat status. Slow-cooked red cabbage, sharpened up with a little apple and vinegar, is a superb partner for many of the winter's other great dishes. Its colour makes a change, for a start; and the piquant taste and succulence of a good braised red cabbage is the perfect counterpoint to strong gamey meats like hare, pheasant and venison. Throw in some cooked chestnuts and it's even nicer.

Braising red cabbage is simple: it needs to be chopped finely, seasoned with salt and pepper (and optional nutmeg, cinnamon and cloves) then cooked in a low oven for an hour or so with chopped cooking apple and onion. Together with the apples, stirring in a shot of vinegar at the end helps to preserve the cabbage's colour, which can otherwise wash out to a less appealing blue; and adding a little sugar rounds out the flavour even more. For other seasonal cabbage treats, see also spring greens (*p. 63*) and savoy cabbage (*p. 40*). And for an overview, there's a cabbage seasonality table on p. 63.

Celeriac

A warty, pockmarked globe with hairy, dangling roots, celeriac invites you to run away screaming rather than welcome it into your kitchen. It is perhaps for this reason that celeriac has only recently become more popular in Britain for its excellent flavour and seasonal fit with other produce of the cold months.

Celeriac, which, along with celery (*see below*) and leaf celery is one of three edible forms assumed by the vegetable *Apium graveolens*, is a slow-growing plant, maturing in the autumn and winter. The bit we eat is not a root but, as with swede, a swollen stem-base, or corm. This is used by the plant to store nutrients over the winter, and in the case of celeriac has been encouraged to develop to a size that makes it a decent eating (and commercial) proposition. And the shops are the best place to find celeriac, because it is hard to get it to grow to worthwhile proportions.

Celeriac may look hideous, but it is a welcome and flavoursome part of the winter cooking repertoire. It shares the basic flavour of celery, but is milder and sweeter. This slight piquancy makes it a good partner to the season's game, alongside which it can be roasted. It also makes a good mash or purée, particularly when mixed with potatoes; or if you're feeling a little ascetic it can be grated and eaten raw. Adventurous cooks might want to attempt the classic celeriac rémoulade, in which finely grated celeriac is mixed into mustard-flavoured, home-made mayonnaise.

Celery

It can sometimes be difficult to see the point of celery. At its worst it is tasteless, stringy, watery and evocative of cheerless dieting. But like many things for which seasonality is very important, good celery, eaten at the right time, is a real treat. It was traditionally grown in the rich black soils of the Fens, in a labour-intensive and risky process but one that produces a high-quality product. The winter celery that results is white rather than green, full of Fenland soil and very good to eat. Although English varieties are grown overseas out of season, the now small-scale production of 'traditional' celery is worth seeking out. It is a relatively labour-intensive process because the best type of celery must be 'earthed up' to blanch the stalks so that they achieve a more subtle flavour; and it is risky, because the frosts that improve its flavour can also wipe out a crop.

There's another reason for seeking out celery in its season: it pairs extremely well with other foods that also just happen to be at their peak. Stilton cheese (*see p. 150*) should be in excellent condition in December; raw celery, stilton and the inevitable glass of port make a luxuriously tasty triumvirate.

Celery also does great things when cooked, adding flavour to sauces as well as taking on the flavour of whatever is cooked with it: the recipe (*see p. 149*) for pheasant braised with celery is a perfect example of this. And if you don't fancy the outer, tougher stems, your stockpot most certainly will.

Parsnips

The parsnip has an image problem. Being absent from fashionable Mediterranean cuisine and associated with scarecrows' noses hasn't helped its cause. Its strange, sweet flavour wavers unsteadily between delightful and disturbing, depending on how it is prepared. The parsnip's history hasn't helped it either. It has an association with poverty and shortage – it was used as a substitute staple food when grain harvests were poor – and as one of the few vegetables thought native to Britain, it always lacked the glamour and novelty of imported varieties.

Treated properly, and eaten in season, the parsnip has much to offer. It is a slow-growing root, flowering in the spring and summer and becoming ready to harvest in the autumn and winter. It is always worth waiting until after the first frosts before eating parsnip, for frost converts more of its starches into sugars and improves the quality. Parsnips are extremely hardy and will stay in the ground through the worst of winter weather until needed, making them a reliable winter staple. It was for this reason, together with their sweetness, that the cultivation of parsnips was originally popular: they preceded potatoes as a staple winter food in Britain and their boiled juice was even used as a substitute for expensive honey. Jane Grigson notes that in the Second World War cooked parsnips were flavoured with banana essence in a vain attempt to mimic the much-missed exotic fruit. Thankfully we don't have to do such things with parsnips today.

How to get the best out of them? Parsnips are famously good roasted or turned into chips, because their skins caramelize deliciously to contrast well with the sweet pulpy interior. Resist the temptation to peel them, because much of the goodness lies just beneath the skin. They go particularly well with beef, especially when roasted alongside the joint; and have a surprising affinity with white fish. Bizarrely, because of their sugar content, parsnips also make excellent wine.

There should be no problem getting hold of parsnips in Britain. East Anglia has the combination of light soils and winter cold that produces the perfect parsnip. Organic parsnips are likely to be sown later (to avoid carrot root fly) so will be very much a vegetable for the depths of winter. If you grow your own, the flowers attract beneficial insects, particularly honey bees: a sweet partner for a sweet vegetable.

Pheasant

One can't help feeling sorry for pheasant. Tales of their stupidity are legion and their lack of traffic sense is attested to by the grim quantities of roadkill that line the lanes near country estates in the shooting season. Pheasants are fated to fly, rather incompetently, in a straight line, making them the perfect quarry for a sozzled toff. Still, if they weren't such popular game birds it is unlikely that pheasants would be so abundant in Britain. As it is, with the season kicking off on 1 October, pheasant makes a welcome addition to the autumn culinary repertoire.

Be aware, though, that pheasant is not truly wild game. Most will have started life in conditions similar to free-range chicken before being released to face the guns. So there is an argument that suggests waiting awhile before buying your pheasant: the ones that have made it to the end of October and beyond will at least have had a bit of exercise and may consequently be tastier.

A good pheasant is a wonderful thing. It must be hung in order to develop its flavour: Jane Grigson suggests a hard stare at the butcher to determine whether this has been done. Younger birds give plenty of meat and roast well, as long as they are well larded. Accompanied by the season's chestnuts and spuds, pheasant is a fine roast dinner. Older, stringier birds are good for rich stews and braises.

Pheasant braised with celery
In this recipe adapted from Jane Grigson's English Food, *the celery enriches the pheasant's flavour while also becoming soft and succulent with the bird's juices.*

1 pheasant	300ml/1/2 pint stock
a knob of butter	1 head of celery
1 onion, chopped	salt and freshly ground pepper
3 rashers unsmoked bacon,	1 egg yolk and 300ml/1/2 pint
cut into strips	double cream (optional)
1 glass of port	

Melt the butter and brown the pheasant in it together with the chopped onion. Put the bird breast-side down in an ovenproof dish with the onion.

Add the strips of bacon to a saucepan with the port and the stock, bring to the boil then pour over the pheasant. Cover the dish with a lid or double layer of foil and put it into the oven for 30 minutes at 180°C/350°F/gas 4.

Clean and finely slice the head of celery, then remove the pheasant from the oven, turn it right side up in the pot and pack it around, inside and underneath, with the celery. Season well. Return to the oven for a further 30 minutes or so.

At this point you can serve it, for it is delicious. Or, for extra decadence, beat together the egg yolk and cream, mix this with the cooking liquor and thicken it on a gentle heat to create a rich sauce.

Serves 4.

Stilton

We like to eat Stilton at Christmas, but isn't that simply because it legitimizes the consumption of vast quantities of port? That is a factor, of course; but there is a minor seasonal dimension to the cheese. Stilton is widely available, all year round. Like all cheeses, its character and quality are dependent on the milk from which it is made; and Stilton needs a lot of milk, with 72 litres/16 gallons going into one 7.5kg/16lb cheese. And the character of the milk, which in the case of Stilton is taken from cows in Derbyshire, Leicestershire and Nottinghamshire, depends upon what the cows have been eating. The process of making Stilton takes from six to fifteen weeks, so by Christmas some of it will come from cows that are eating winter fodder rather than fresh grass. This gives an extra richness to the cheese that further justifies its place as a luxurious dessert cheese for the festive season. The same applies to the rarer blue Wensleydale cheese, also worth seeking out for its mid-winter quality.

Turkey

Turkeys divide gourmets. There are many who shun them for their sometimes bland, dry meat; they seek racier, tastier Christmas alternatives such as goose (*see p. 111*), or a costly joint of meat. There's no reason for a turkey not to provide a fine roast: a bird of a good breed, such as a Bronze or a Norfolk Black, that has been reared humanely and hung after slaughter for a couple of weeks, should make excellent eating. The reason for turkey's being sniffed at as a seasonal delicacy today is likely to have more to do with the industrialization of turkey farming over the last thirty or so years.

Despite its transatlantic origin, turkey does have a relatively long heritage as a Christmas meal in Britain, having been cited as festive fare from the sixteenth century onwards. Turkey farming centred on Cambridgeshire and Norfolk, where it fitted in perfectly with the area's drier climate, and the annual cycle of its cereal crops. Like geese, turkeys were driven down to London after harvest, feeding as they went on the gleanings from fields of stubble. Although it is a long time now since turkey drovers plied their trade, it is only quite recently that turkey farming has become so mechanized.

Turkeys are aggressive, disease-prone and difficult to look after. However, with the use of drugs and climate- and light-controlled housing, they can be reared in large densities, with one person managing up to 25,000 birds. In both intensive and less high-tech indoor systems, there is much concern for turkey welfare: for example, the birds are bred for a weight of breast meat that can lead to leg injuries and which prevents them mating naturally. As a result, in such systems it is someone's job (not mine, thankfully) to 'milk' male turkeys for semen. This intensive production results in the dry, bland, low-cost 'white' turkey that is available all year round (of the 35 million turkeys killed each year, only 10 million are for the Christmas market). The better breeds tend to be reared specifically for Christmas, so if you're a gourmet who happens to like turkey, it really is worth waiting for the season and paying the premium for the most free-range bird you can find.

Woodcock

Small, attractive, peaceful-looking creatures, woodcock don't seem to deserve their traditional gastronomic fate. Like other game birds, they have a tightly controlled and relatively short season during which they can be shot legally: in the case of woodcock this runs from the beginning of October (September in Scotland) to the end of January. For the rest of the year, they are protected so that the species can breed, spread out and raise young in peace – at least until the autumn comes around again.

Woodcock is a seasonal treat, and a very tempting one; Alan Davidson notes that the bird 'eats a varied diet of wholesome foods and presents a plump aspect'. Its numbers are boosted in the winter by migrant birds, who were once believed to spend the other part of the year on the moon, a notion that is no longer current. As for many things, it is worth waiting a little while into the season before seeking out woodcock, so that they will have had time to get some exercise and eat their fill of autumnal delicacies.

The compact elegance of a woodcock belies the visceral experience of eating one in the customary way. They are cooked with their guts (or 'trail') still inside, for woodcock defecate on takeoff, so their insides are always clean when the bird flies into the line of fire. The trail is traditionally spread on toast to accompany the bird. The woodcock's head is left on while it is roasted, so that its long beak can be used as a handy skewer to keep the bird together in the oven. The head is then served neatly bisected, so that the tiny brains can be eaten with a tiny spoon. Eating woodcock is, therefore, the subject of a wee bit of machismo; cooking it even more so. But it is worth the effort, for its meat has a rich, intense gaminess and its offal is equally delightful. This quality will at least in part be due to the fact that woodcock is truly wild, unlike pheasant (*see p. 149*), much of which will have been reared artificially before release.

A costly, ceremonial late-autumn and winter dish, woodcock turns up in specialist butchers, game dealers and at good restaurants: it is something every seasonal gourmet should try if the (rare) opportunity presents itself.

Year Planner

	January	February	March
Meat	Goose Hare Mallard Partridge Pheasant Rabbit Snipe Venison Woodcock	Hare Mallard Partridge Pheasant Rabbit Venison	Rabbit Venison
Fruit and nuts	Apples Pears Rhubarb, forced	Apples Pears Rhubarb, forced	Apples Pears Rhubarb, forced
Fish	Mussels Oysters, native Scallops Turbot	Mussels Oysters, native Scallops Turbot	Mussels Oysters, native Salmon, wild Scallops Elvers
Vegetables and mushrooms	Artichoke, Jerusalem Beetroot Broccoli, purple sprouting Brussels sprouts Cabbages Carrots Cauliflower Celeriac Chard Chicory and endive Garlic Kale Kohlrabi Leeks Lettuce Onions Parsnip Potatoes Salsify, scorzonera Spinach Squash Swede Turnips	Artichoke, Jerusalem Beetroot Broccoli, purple sprouting Brussels sprouts Cabbages Carrots Cauliflower Celeriac Chard Chicory and endive Garlic Kale Kohlrabi Leeks Lettuce Onions Parsnips Potatoes Salsify, scorzonera Spinach Squash Swede Turnips	Beetroot Broccoli, purple sprouting Brussels sprouts Cabbages Cauliflower Chard Chicory and endive Garlic Kale Leeks Lettuce Nettles Onions Onions, spring Parsnips Potatoes Radishes Seakale Sorrel Spinach Squash Turnips
Cheese	Stilton Wensleydale, blue	Stilton Wensleydale, blue	Ewe's milk cheeses Stilton

• **Seasonal treat** • New in season • **In season** • **Last month** • **From store**

	April	*May*	*June*
Meat	Venison Wood pigeon	Lamb, new season Rook Venison Wood pigeon	Lamb, new season Venison Wood pigeon
Fruit and nuts	Apples Rhubarb, outdoor	Apples Elderflowers Rhubarb, outdoor	Apples Blackcurrants Cherries Elderflowers Gooseberrries Loganberries Raspberries Redcurrants Rhubarb, outdoor
Fish	Crab, brown Elvers Lobster Oysters, native Salmon, wild Sea trout Turbot	Crab, brown Herring Lobster Salmon, wild Sea trout Turbot	Crab, brown Herring Lobster Mackerel Salmon, wild Sea trout Turbot
Vegetables and mushrooms	Broccoli, purple sprouting Cabbages Cauliflower Chard Dandelion Endive Garlic Garlic, wild Lettuce Mushrooms, morel Nettles Onions Onions, spring Potatoes Potatoes Radishes Seakale Sorrel Spinach Spring greens Turnips Watercress	Asparagus Beans, broad Beetroot Cabbages Cauliflower Chard Dandelion Endive Garlic Lettuce Mushrooms, morel Nettles Onions Onions, spring Peas Potatoes Radishes Rocket, wild Seakale Sorrel Spinach Spring greens Turnips Watercress	Artichokes, globe Asparagus Beans, broad Beetroot Broccoli, calabrese Cabbages Carrots Cauliflower Chard Cucumber Dandelion Endive Garlic Lettuce Onions Onions, spring Peas Potatoes Radishes Rocket, wild Samphire Sorrel Spinach Spring greens Turnips Watercress
Cheese	Ewe's milk cheeses	Ewe's milk cheeses Stinking Bishop	Ewe's milk cheeses Goat's milk cheese, fresh Stinking Bishop

• **Seasonal treat** • New in season • **In season** • **Last month** • **From store**

	July	August	September
Meat	Lamb, new season Venison Wood pigeon	Grouse Lamb, new season Ptarmigan Snipe Venison Wood pigeon	Goose Grouse Hare Lamb, new season Mallard Partridge Ptarmigan Rabbit Snipe Venison Wood pigeon
Fruit and nuts	Blackcurrants Blueberries Cherries Elderflowers Gooseberrries Loganberries Raspberries Redcurrants Rhubarb, outdoor Strawberries	Apples Blackberries Blackcurrants Blueberries Cherries Cobnuts Loganberries Pears Plums Raspberries Redcurrants Strawberries	Apples Plums Blackberries Raspberries Blackcurrants Redcurrants Blueberries Sloes Chestnuts Strawberries Cobnuts Walnuts Crabapples Damsons, bullaces Elderberries Loganberries Pears
Fish	Bream, black Crab, brown Herring Lobster Mackerel Salmon, wild Sea trout Turbot	Bream, black Crab, brown Herring Lobster Mackerel Salmon, wild Sea trout Turbot	Bream, black Crab, brown Herring Eel Lobster Mackerel Mussels Oysters, native Sea trout Turbot

Vegetables and mushrooms	Artichokes, globe Onions, spring
	Beans, broad Peas
	Beans, French Potatoes
	Beans, runner Radishes
	Beetroot Rocket, wild
	Broccoli, calabrese Samphire
	Cabbages Shallots
	Carrots Sorrel
	Cauliflower Spinach
	Chard Turnips
	Cucumber Watercress
	Dandelion
	Endive
	Fennel
	Garlic
	Kohlrabi
	Lettuce
	Onions
		Artichokes, globe Leeks
		Aubergines Lettuce
		Beans, broad Mushrooms, wild
		Beans, French Onions
		Beans, runner Onions, spring
		Beetroot Peas
		Broccoli, calabrese Potatoes
		Cabbages Pumpkins
		Carrots Radishes
		Cauliflower Rocket, wild
		Chard Samphire
		Courgettes Shallots
		Cucumber Sorrel
		Dandelion Spinach
		Endive Squash
		Fennel Sweetcorn
		Garlic Tomatoes
		Kohlrabi Turnips
		  Watercress
			Artichokes, globe Kohlrabi
			Aubergines Leeks
			Beans, broad Lettuce
			Beans, French Mushrooms, wild
			Beans, runner Onions
			Beetroot Onions, spring
			Broccoli, calabrese Peas
			Cabbages Potatoes
			Carrots Pumpkins
			Cauliflower Rocket, wild
			Chard Samphire
			Courgettes Sorrel
			Cucumber Spinach
			Dandelion Squash
			Endive Swede
			Fennel Sweetcorn
			Garlic Tomatoes
			Kale Turnips
			  Watercress

Cheese	Goat's milk cheese, fresh Stinking Bishop	Goat's milk cheese, fresh	

154

• **Seasonal treat** • New in season • **In season** • **Last month** • **From store**

	October	November	December
Meat	Goose Grouse Hare Lamb, new season Mallard Partridge Pheasant Ptarmigan Rabbit Snipe Squirrel, grey Venison Woodcock **Wood pigeon**	Goose Grouse Hare **Lamb, new season** Mallard Partridge Pheasant Ptarmigan Rabbit Snipe Squirrel, grey Venison Woodcock	Goose **Grouse** Hare Mallard Partridge Pheasant **Ptarmigan** Rabbit Snipe **Squirrel, grey** Turkey Venison Woodcock
Fruit and nuts	Apples **Blackberries** **Blueberries** Chestnuts Crabapples Damsons, bullaces **Elderberries** **Loganberries** Medlars Pears **Plums** Quinces **Raspberries** Sloes **Walnuts**	**Apples** Chestnuts Medlars Pears Quinces Sloes	Apples Chestnuts Pears Quinces
Fish	Bream, black **Crab, brown** Herring Eel Lobster Mackerel Mussels Oysters, native Turbot	Bream, black Herring **Lobster** **Mackerel** Mussels Oysters, native Turbot	Bream, black Herring Mussels Oysters, native Turbot
Vegetables and mushrooms	Artichokes, Jerusalem **Aubergines** **Beans, runner** Beetroot **Broccoli, calabrese** Brussels sprouts Cabbages Cardoon Carrots Cauliflower Celeriac Celery Chard Chicory **Courgettes** **Cucumber** Endive Fennel Garlic Kale Kohlrabi Leeks Lettuce Mushrooms, wild Onions Onions, spring Parsnips Potatoes Pumpkins **Rocket, wild** Salsify, scorzonera Sorrel Spinach Squash Swede **Tomatoes** Turnips	Artichokes, Jerusalem **Beetroot** **Brussels sprouts** Cabbages Cardoon Carrots Cauliflower Celeriac Celery Chard Chicory Endive Garlic Kale Kohlrabi Leeks Lettuce **Mushrooms, wild** Onions Onions, spring Parsnips Potatoes Pumpkins Salsify, scorzonera **Sorrel** Spinach Squash Swede Turnips	Artichokes, Jerusalem **Beetroot** **Brussels sprouts** Cabbages **Cardoon** Carrots Cauliflower Celeriac Celery Chard Chicory Endive **Garlic** Kale Kohlrabi Leeks Lettuce Onions Onions, spring Parsnips Potatoes Pumpkins Salsify, scorzonera Spinach Squash Swede Turnips
Cheese			Stilton Wensleydale, blue

• **Seasonal treat** • New in season • In season • **Last month** • **From store**

Suppliers and further information
Where to find seasonal food
Abel & Cole
organic fruit and veg delivery throughout the UK, with a focus on British seasonal produce
www.abel-cole.co.uk
Farm Retail Association
comprehensive listing of farms throughout Britain that sell their produce direct
www.farmshopping.com
National Association of Farmers' Markets
contains an up-to-date listing of farmers' markets throughout Britain
www.farmersmarkets.net
Organic Butchers' Guide
a guide to where to buy organic meat in Britain
www.organicbutchers.co.uk
WI Country Markets
a guide to the many Women's Institute markets around the country
www.wimarkets.co.uk

Some personal favourite suppliers
A. H. Griffiths
the odd squirrel and rook, and the best bacon in Britain
22 High Street, Leintwardine, nr Craven Arms, Shropshire, 01547 540231
Steve Hatt
superb fish 88–90 Essex Road, London N1, 020 7226 3963
Hamish Johnston
fine cheeses
www.hamishjohnston.com
Loch Fyne
seafood, meat and game by mail order
www.loch-fyne.com
M. Moen & Sons
free range and organic meats
www.moen.co.uk
Riverford Organic Vegetables
veg delivered in the south of England and Wales
www.riverford.co.uk

Interesting food-related organizations

Common Ground
charity that champions local diversity; its websites have much information on local events and traditions, many relating to food
www.commonground.org.uk

Marine Conservation Society
contains useful information on which fish species to eat with a clearer conscience
www.mcsuk.org

Slow Food
Italian-based but rapidly growing global movement dedicated to local, sustainable food
www.slowfood.com

Soil Association
campaigning group for organic farming with a wealth of information about food
www.soilassociation.org

Cookery books and British food

Annie Bell's Vegetable Book, Annie Bell, Michael Joseph, 1997

The British Housewife, Martha Bradley, first published 1756, facsimile edition published by Prospect Books, 1998

English Food, Jane Grigson, Penguin, first published 1974, revised edition published 1992

500 Recipes for Jams, Pickles, Chutneys, Marguerite Patten, Paul Hamlyn, 1963

Food in England, Dorothy Hartley, first published 1954, published by Little, Brown 1999

Four Seasons Cookery Book, Margaret Costa, first published 1970, new edition published by Grub Street, 1999

Good Things, Jane Grigson, Penguin Books, 1973

How to Eat, Nigella Lawson, Chatto & Windus, 1998

The River Café Cook Book Green, Rose Gray and Ruth Rogers, Ebury Press, 2000

The River Cottage Year, Hugh Fearnley-Whittingstall, Hodder & Stoughton, 2003

Traditional Foods of Britain, Laura Mason and Catherine Brown, Prospect Books, 1999

Food politics and history

British Food: an extraordinary thousand years of history, Colin Spencer, Grub Street, 2002

Captive State, George Monbiot, Macmillan, 2000

Cottage Economy, William Cobbett, first published in book form 1822, published by Oxford University Press 1979

Fast Food Nation, Eric Schlosser, Penguin, 2001
Food: a history, Felipe Fernandez-Armesto, Macmillan, 2001
The Food We Eat, Joanna Blythman, Michael Joseph 1996
The Killing of the Countryside, Graham Harvey, Vintage, 1998
So Shall We Reap, Colin Tudge, Penguin, 2003

Growing your own

The Complete Book of Self-Sufficiency, John Seymour, Dorling Kindersley, 1976
Encyclopaedia of Organic Gardening, Henry Doubleday Research Association, editor-in-chief
     Pauline Pears, Dorling Kindersley, 2001
Fork to Fork, Monty and Sarah Don, Conran Octopus, 1999
The River Cottage Cookbook, Hugh Fearnley-Whittingstall, HarperCollins, 2001

Reference

The Book of Apples, Joan Morgan and Alison Richards, Ebury Press, 1993
Fish, Sophie Grigson and William Black, Headline, 1998
Good Fish Guide, Bernadette Clarke, Marine Conservation Society, 2002
Leith's Seasonal Bible, C. J. Jackson and Be Kassapian, Bloomsbury, 1998
Mushrooms and Other Fungi of Great Britain, Roger Phillips, Pan, 1981
The Oxford Companion to Food, Alan Davidson, Oxford University Press, 1999
Vegetables, Roger Phillips and Martyn Rix, Pan, 1993

Weather and climate

Climate of the British Isles, T. J Chandler and S. Gregory, Longman, 1976
March Winds and April Showers: country weather lore, Ralph Whitlock, Ex Libris, 1993
Nature through the Seasons, Richard Adams, Penguin, 1976
Weather, David Ludlum, HarperCollins, 2001
Weather and Agriculture, J. A. Taylor (ed.), Pergamon, 1967

Wild food

Britain's Wild Harvest, Hew D. V. Prendergast and Helen Sanderson, Royal Botanic Gardens,
     Kew and the Countryside Agency, 2004
A Cook on the Wild Side, Hugh Fearnley-Whittingstall, Boxtree, 1997
Food for Free, Richard Mabey, HarperCollins, 1972
Wild Food, Roger Phillips, Pan, 1983

Miscellany

A Cook's Tour: global adventures in extreme cuisines, Anthony Bourdain, Ecco, 2000
It Must Have Been Something I Ate, Jeffrey Steingarten, Headline, 2002
Straw Dogs, John Gray, Granta, 2002